MW01101629

Da Bonnie Isle

Da Bonnie Isle

Whalsay through the ages

James A. Anderson

The Shetland Times Ltd.,
Lerwick
2021

Da Bonnie Isle

Whalsay through the ages

First published by The Shetland Times Ltd., 2021.

© James A. Anderson, 2021.

ISBN 978-1-910997-34-5

All rights reserved.

No part of this publication may be reproduced, stored in a retrieval system, or transmitted, in any form, by any means, electronic, mechanical, photocopying, recording or otherwise, without the prior written permission of the publishers.

James Anderson has asserted his right under the Copyright, Design and Patents Act 1988, to be identified as Author of this Work.

A catalogue record for this book is available from the British Library.

Printed and published by
The Shetland Times Ltd.,
Gremista,
Lerwick,
Shetland,
Scotland, ZE1 0PX.

For my late parents
Gilbert from Whitefield (1903 - 1978)
and Robina (Beenie) from Brough (1903 - 2007).

Contents

Acknowledgements

I would like to acknowledge and thank the following people for assisting me with the research for this book and providing illustrations. Firstly, the members of the Whalsay History Group at the Heritage Centre without whose help I would not have got past the first page. The amount of information about Whalsay that they have amassed over the years is amazing and their ability to find their way through it all to get me the information I needed equally so. They were: Marina Irvine, Jacqueline Irvine, Hazel Sales, Ruby Poleson, Jeanette Wishart, Lilian Eunson, David Williamson, Larry Williamson, Andy Sandison, and Peter Hughson. They also provided me with a memory stick full of excellent photos to illustrate the book and for that I am particularly indebted to Marina.

John Lowrie Jamieson edited my original draft of the section on shipwrecks, a subject he has been collecting information on for years. He was also instrumental in identifying the possible site of a Viking water mill at Stiki's Burn when he discovered that "stiki" meant "dam" in Old Norse, not a man's name as had previously been thought.

Dodie Poleson, pioneering shareholder in the *Serene* and her replacements, provided his depth of knowledge on the fishing industry.

Rosie Williamson provided information on births and deaths and drew my attention to two deaths of fishermen at sea which I had initially omitted.

Staff at the Shetland Islands Council's Archives, Brian Smith and Angus Johnson provided additional information and advice. The chapter on the Hanseatic merchants is based on research carried out by Brian Smith. Ian Tait at the Shetland Museum was a useful source of information on archaeological matters and other more recent events including the likely origin of the Pier House and the Hame Dock. Ian's book on *Shetland's Vernacular Buildings* also solved a puzzle which I had not been able to find an answer to in

Da Bonnie Isle

Whalsay – when did plantie crubs appear in the landscape? Jenny Murray, Curator of Collections at the Shetland Museum, provided a list of all archaeological artefacts held in the museum with useful notes about each of them. Janet Smith (neé Barclay) provided me with a web-site reference to get into the entrails of the Scottish Listed Buildings and Structures records.

Magnie Jamieson provided an excellent photo of the old *Research* at sea. The 1986 photo of the massed ranks of Whalsay fishermen posing with Henry Stewart down at the harbour, which Henry wanted to use in his campaign at Shetland Islands Council for money to be allocated for the final phase of harbour works, was by Dennis Coutts. The photograph of the sixareen *Vaila Mae* under sail is by Dave Donaldson. Ian Reid provided the photograph of the new *Serene*, and the cover image.

1

Introduction

The island of Whalsay, known as Da Bonnie Isle in the local dialect, is one of the North Isles group in the Shetland Islands, measuring just five and a half miles by two. The name comes from the Old Norse language's word for Whale Island – Hvalsoy. Seen in profile from the sea approaching from the east, the island looks like a whale, the 393 feet high Wart o' Clate at the south end tapering away to the peninsula of Skaw Taing at the north end.

The settlement of the island goes back well over 5,000 years to the Neolithic (New Stone Age) period and there are substantial archaeological sites dating from this period and the later Bronze and Iron Ages. The Picts were around when the Vikings arrived from south-west Norway before 800AD, their name preserved in the Viking name for a Neolithic chambered burial cairn between Skaw and Isbister at Pettisgarthsfield.

Whalsay was an important base for the German Hanseatic merchants who controlled trade with Shetland from the early middle ages to the beginning of the 18th century. The Hamburg merchants' booth, the Pier House, has now been restored as a museum to the trade and the Bremen Booth is now a private house standing just above the Pier House.

In 1469 Shetland was put up as surety against a dowry being paid by the King of Norway to the King of Scotland for the Norwegian's daughter. Since the dowry was never paid, the islands became Scottish by default. In the 16th century, Scottish noble families moved in, taking over ownership of the land from the former owners, the peerie (small) lairds, often by underhand means. Whalsay was taken over by the Bruces of Symbister, descendants of Robert the Bruce's family line. Their original home, the Auld Haa, is now a private house. Their later Georgian mansion, the Haa or Symbister House, has been converted into the secondary school. Whalsay is

Map of
Shetland

Muckle Flugga

Hermaness   Skaw

Haroldswick
Baltasound
UNST
Gloup
Cullivoe   Uyeasound
Belmont
Gutcher
Sellafirth

Uyea

North   Mid Yell   FETLAR
Roe   West   Tresta Funzie
Sandwick
YELL Aywick
Ronas Hill

Eshaness   Ollaberry
Ulsta   Burravoe   OUT
Hillswick   SKERRIES
Toft
Sullom   Mossbank

Lunna

Brae

PAPA   Vidlin
STOUR   Muckle Roe   Voe Laxo
WHALSAY
Symbister

Sandness   West   Nesting
Burrafirth   Aith
Bixter   MAINLAND

Walls   Weisdale
Whiteness
Vaila   Skeld   Tingwall
FOULA

Lerwick   NOSS
Scalloway
Gulberwick
Trondra
East Burra   Quarff   BRESSAY

West Burra   Cunningsburgh

Sandwick

Bigton   Levenwick

Boddam
Dunrossness
Quendale   Grutness
Sumburgh Head

FAIR
ISLE

From Aberdeen 211 m (338km)
From Orkney (Kirkwall) 115m (185km)

Grutness to
Fair Isle
24m (40km)

the leading fishing community in Shetland with a large fleet of whitefish boats, seven large pelagic trawlers pursuing herring and mackerel and some smaller boats involved in the shellfish sector. This tradition of commercial fishing goes back to Hanseatic times when dried, salted cod and ling, known as stockfish, was the main export of the Germans. After the Germans had gone, a type of fishing, called haaf fishing developed, using bigger boats (sixareens) in deeper water – up to fifty miles from land – and controlled by the lairds. After some fishing disasters in the 19th century, particularly the disaster of 1881, when many boats and lives were lost, the haaf fishing declined and many parts of Shetland abandoned their fishing activities. However, Whalsay persevered, adopting bigger, decked boats and fishing for herring in the summer months.

Whalsay avoided the clearances of crofters off the land by lairds to make way for extensive sheep farming which occurred in other parts of Shetland in the 19th century and was thus able to preserve its population.

At the time of the 1861 population census, when Shetland's population peaked at over 31,000, Whalsay had 728 people. In 1961, when Shetland bottomed out at 17,812, Whalsay had 872. By 2011 it had grown to 1,061.

In the 1950s, Whalsay had not changed much from Victorian times as far as daily life went. It was still pretty much self-sufficient subsistence living from the products of the croft and fishing. Piped water didn't arrive until 1953. There were few cars and transport into and out of the island was by coastal steamer, the *Earl of*

Map of Whalsay

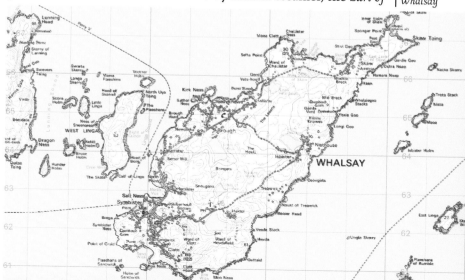

WHALSAY

Zetland. Electricity and hence television didn't come until 1963. Sewerage schemes had to wait until oil money enabled the Shetland Islands Council to construct a programme of schemes in the 1980s and 1990s.

Shetland Charitable Trust money provided a leisure centre with a swimming pool and a care centre. Starting in the 1960s, harbour works produced a fine harbour sheltered by breakwaters. The car ferry service to Laxo and Vidlin transformed communications. There is now talk of a bridge or tunnel to the mainland which would reduce the island's isolation even further.

2

The Neolithic, Bronze
And Iron Ages

Whalsay's first inhabitants arrived well over 5,000 years ago in what is known as the Neolithic (New Stone Age) period. They were farmers cultivating crops, chiefly barley and raising livestock – cattle, sheep and poultry – later also pigs. Agriculture developed in the Fertile Crescent of the Middle East, centred on the valleys of the Tigris and Euphrates Rivers and gradually spread west into Europe as some people migrated west and as their techniques were adopted by existing groups of people. It is not known precisely where in Europe the people who reached Shetland came from, although a progression along the Atlantic seaboard from the Mediterranean is a favoured theory.

No archaeological evidence of the type of boats they used has been preserved but something along the lines of the Irish curragh is likely, a timber frame covered with animal skins. The climate at the time was warmer and sea conditions would probably have been better than at present. Whalsay would have had a substantial mixed deciduous tree cover at the time with birch, rowan, willow, hazel and juniper and fertile brown-earth soils. The peat along the Muckle Burn, which runs through the central valley from the Huxter Loch to the North Voe, contains the remains of tree roots six inches in diameter. Research on pollen from bore holes taken during harbour work at Symbister in the 1960s and elsewhere in Shetland has identified that the islands were well wooded at this time, open woodland being characteristic with tree and shrub pollen amounting to up to 70% of the total. (See Simon Butler's article in *The Shaping of Shetland*, Editor Val Turner.) The remains of Neolithic dwellings can be seen all over the island in places where there are no longer houses, suggesting a substantial population, as sites in the current settlements would have been obliterated.

With a warmer climate and before the peat cover developed, places higher above sea level were obviously suitable for settlement and cultivation. In Neolithic times, Orkney appears to have been an important centre of the culture with a large temple complex being excavated at the Ness of Brodgar which pre-dated Stonehenge and may have pioneered the practise of erecting stone circles of that type elsewhere in Britain. Shetland may therefore not have been on the periphery of things then.

The best-known Neolithic house sites are below the hill called Pettisgarthsfield between Isbister and Skaw, the Benie House and the Stones of Yoxie. The Benie House is an example of the clover-leaf style of Neolithic house. Alcoves set into the walls would have served as sleeping areas. The entrances have narrow porches. Better preserved houses at Jarlshof in Sumburgh have protruding flat topped stones used as dressers and a central hearth, smoke from which would have escaped through a hole in the roof. It is assumed that roofs would have been of turf or heather supported by beams of whale bone or timber. The foundations of other houses can be seen all over the island, often among groups of plantie crubs (See 7, Agriculture) which have obviously been built using stones from the Neolithic houses.

Sandy Simpson from Houll, who was born in 1900, could remember when he was a small boy seeing plantie crubs being built at the Houll Loch from the remains of Neolithic houses. A clear illustration of this process remains as shown in the photograph. Other examples are at the Sandwick Loch, east of Nuckrawater, and west of Buwater. Another site, not pillaged for plantie crubs, is below the rocky crag known as the Water Hammars south of the Huxter Loch. Just outside the croft at Whitefield there is a Neolithic house foundation and nearby a cist type grave. Two more Neolithic graves can be seen on hilltops in the Sneugins, the hills which run along the northern side of the island's central valley. Traces of a stone wall can be seen starting near this house site and traceable all the way to the Loch of Livister. The foundation of another wall runs between the Huxter Loch and Buwater. These are thought to have been the boundaries between land

The Benie Hoose – Neolithic dwelling.

Chambered Cairn Bronze Age burial at Pettigarthsfield.

Neolithic cist burial chamber at Whitefield.

Bronze Age burned mound at Sandwick Loch.

Stone circle at Sandwick Loch.

Neolithic house and plantie crub at Houll Loch.

holdings of different groups of people possibly similar to the scattald fences or hill-dykes of today.

Above the Benie House, on Pettigarthsfield, there is a small heel-shaped burial cairn grave site, five metres in diameter, enclosing a central chamber a metre wide, with a cist type grave just to the north. Another chambered cairn burial site is on the Wart of Symbister. A one and a half-metre-tall standing stone, characteristic of Neolithic culture, can be seen at Skaw with two fallen stones alongside and two more upright stones near the road down to Pouster.

The Bronze Age in Shetland is taken to run from around 1800BC to 600BC. By this time the climate had deteriorated with colder, wetter conditions developing, possibly associated with a period of volcanic activity in Iceland creating "nuclear winter" conditions. The tree cover had largely gone, Neolithic settlers having cleared it for cultivation, firewood and construction and animals inhibiting re-growth by grazing on young shoots. The soil had become more acidic with peat cover developing. In Whalsay, settlement contracted down to the coastal strip, similar to the present pattern. Whether new people arrived or just new ideas, some significant cultural changes occurred. Firstly, burnt mounds appear, illustrating a new form of cooking. These horseshoe-shaped piles of burnt stones containing a water trough are believed to have been used to cook food as an alternative to roasting. Other theories are that they were saunas or used to dye skins or woollen cloth but the cooking theory seems the most plausible. They are found near sources of fresh water like lochs and burns and adjacent to settlements. The best examples in Whalsay are at the Loch of Sandwick where there are two but nine are shown on the map in Noel Fojut's *Prehistoric and Viking Shetland*, including ones at Challister and Isbister. Whether they were in everyday use or only used for communal festival occasions like weddings is unknown. Just to the south of the largest burnt mound at Sandwick, the stone foundations of two circular features can be seen. The smaller one has been identified in records kept by the local history group as a homestead. It is larger than the Benie House or Yoxli and doesn't have the characteristic porch entrance but Ian Tait, the Shetland

Museum Curator, is of the view that it is just a Neolithic house as there are examples of structures this size elsewhere in Shetland and many of these houses do not have the porch feature. The larger feature is on the scale of the stone circle in Orkney known as the Ring of Brodgar. It is mentioned in the Inventory of Ancient Monuments held in the Shetland Islands Council's Archives but does not appear to have been investigated or written about by anyone, including John Stewart, a keen local amateur archaeologist and historian.

A second cultural change in the Bronze Age was the introduction of cremation in burials. John Stewart has identified two urn burials in steatite urns, one at Vevoe and another on the East Knowe of Setter Hill at Marrister. Steatite was quarried at Catpund near Cunninsburgh but there are also deposits on Whalsay so the urns could either have been locally produced or imported from Catpund. No examples of the new metal after which the Bronze Age has been named have been found in Whalsay.

The Iron Age in Shetland is characterised by the brochs, tall, drystone built towers of which well-preserved examples survive at Clickimin in Lerwick and Mousa. These defensive structures with narrow entrances herald an era of social instability with communities in fear of attack reminiscent of Maori pas in New Zealand which were used in inter-tribal warfare. It seems likely that brochs had a similar function. There were two in Whalsay at Brough and Saltness with a fort on the Loch of Huxter. Logic would suggest that if they were aimed at an external threat one would have sufficed the island. By the time of the Iron Age, the climate and soils had deteriorated further and the large population which had built up in more favourable conditions may have struggled to survive in the face of reducing resources of food, leading to conflict. This was what happened in New Zealand leading to the development of the pa fortresses and in Easter Island.

The fort on a small islet in the Loch of Huxter, connected to the shore by a causeway, was a substantial building, its blockhouse standing two metres tall with an upper gallery in the wall. A wall one and a half metres thick surrounded the islet. Stones from the fort were taken to build the school across the Huxter Loch at Livister in 1864, but substantial ruins remain. A similar fate met the broch at Brough where nothing remains but the name. Its stones were used by the laird to build the strip of twelve new houses in the 1840s. Likewise, only the site of the broch at Saltness can be seen now. As for the Bronze Age, no artefacts using the new metal for which the Iron Age is named have been found in Whalsay. The period during which the brochs were being built and in use seems to have been relatively short, starting around 100BC and ending in the second half of the 2nd century AD.

The Shetland museum holds a number of archaeological artefacts dated to the Neolithic, Bronze and Iron Ages. These include loom weights, polished axes, hammers, pots and pottery sherds. Two Neolithic "Shetland knives", a cutting tool unique to Shetland, have also been found.

Iron Age fort on Loch of Huxter.

3

The Vikings

The Vikings gave Whalsay its name, Whale Island. They arrived before 800AD from south-west Norway in their superbly seaworthy galleys. The fate of their predecessors in the islands, who they called Picts, is not known but their first appearance elsewhere in Britain at Lindisfarne in Northumberland where they slaughtered and robbed the monks in 793AD suggests that the Picts may have suffered a similar fate. The St Ninian's Isle treasure found buried at the former chapel there was probably buried to protect it from the Vikings. The fact that it wasn't seen again until 1958 tells its own story. So does DNA profiling which shows most native Shetland males with Scandinavian ancestry. The picture for females is less clear which suggests that they may have been spared and inter-married with the invaders. In Whalsay, the only clue that the Picts were ever there lies in the place name Pettigarthsfield.

Very few Viking Age houses have been excavated in Shetland and none on Whalsay. The main reason for this is that the pattern of Norse settlement coincided with the present pattern and later houses would have been built on the sites of Viking houses as can be seen at Jarlshof. The best example of a Viking house is at Underhoull in Unst. The shape of houses now changed from round or oval to rectangular with byres and barns attached to the end of the residential areas, hence the name long houses. Other structures still existing and probably having their origin in Norse times are boat noosts and water mills. Noosts are rectangular recesses at the top of beaches, often faced up with stones where boats could be hauled up and shored up safe from the reach of tides. A typical Norse water mill used for grinding corn has been restored at Huxter in Sandness. In Whalsay, a burn called Stiki's Burn runs down along the fence bordering the easternmost croft at East Hamister to enter the Muckle Burn flowing through the island's central valley. "Stiki"

Viking water mills at Huxter, Sandness.

Possible water mill site above Traewick.

is the Old Norse word for dam. Just outside the hill gate into the croft a raised bank can be seen and behind it a flat area of grass surrounded by deep heather. This looks very much like the bed of a former loch. The ruins of possible former water mills can be seen elsewhere on the island, for example just below the road north of Traewick on a burn flowing towards the sea from Nuckrawater.

The Shetland Museum hold some artefacts dated to the Viking period which have been found in Whalsay. These include a steatite dish, cup, hanging lamp, loom weights and a fishing weight. A pottery sherd found in a structure being eroded by the sea at Sutherness was originally thought to be from a Neolithic/Bronze Age house but the notes attached to the artefact record by the Shetland Museum state that: "The remains currently visible appear more likely to be a Viking, Norse or Medieval long house." A toy quern stone of steatite, measuring 11.2 centimetres in diameter by 1.5 centimetres thick was found at Brough and has a note attached to it explaining that toys of this type are not uncommon on Viking sites in Shetland though it could date from later.

Christianity became the official religion of the Norse controlled territories in 995AD. John Stewart identifies four chapels on Whalsay at Symbister, Kirkaness, Isbister and Skaw. The one at Skaw was reputedly built by the survivors of a shipwreck around 1500AD but there may well have been continuity of use of the other sites from Pictish times as some Vikings had converted to Christianity before the official adoption of it.

Whalsay's main Viking legacy lies in the place names. Noel Fojut has suggested that early settlement is characterised by place names ending in "by" and "sta/ster" with "bister" names following later. These would include Symbister and Isbister in Whalsay. It has also been suggested that the earliest Norse settlement was in Unst and Fetlar but there is no concrete evidence of that. Norse place names often denote geographical location, the physical character of a place or some speciality practised there. For example, Symbister is the southern farm, Isbister the eastern farm, Skaw a long narrow, flat peninsula and Marister the place where horses were kept. John Stewart's Shetland Place Names is a fascinating source for local

names: Huxter derives from the Old Norse word for a mound –
there were several prehistoric hillocks there, since removed; Livister
means "leavings" – it was the smallest and last occupied of the early
farms; intriguingly, Stewart claims that Challister derives from
the word for tent "tjald" but offers no explanation as to why this
name was applied. Presumably the earliest settlers lived in tents.

The Shetland connection with Norway pioneered by the Vikings
has continued into modern times. Up-Helly-A', the winter fire
festival held in Lerwick in January every year and now in a
number of other parts of Shetland, celebrates this link as well as
the return of the sun after the winter. During the Second World
War, the clandestine movement of small boats across the North
Sea carrying refugees, freedom fighters, undercover agents and
armaments between Norway and Shetland, known as the Shetland Bus, is now commemorated in a museum in Scalloway. In
August 1990, on an initiative from Måløy, a small-town north of
Bergen, Shetland Islands Council joined with them, Esjberg City
Council in Denmark and Aberdeen City Council to set up KIMO,
an environmental organization dedicated to cleaning up North
Sea pollution. The annual Bergen to Shetland yacht race retraces
the path of the Vikings.

4

The Hanseatic Merchants

For several hundred years from the early Middle Ages, Shetland's trade with Europe was dominated by German merchants, members of the Hanseatic League. This was a group of merchants and shipowners from cities along the North Sea and Baltic coasts which in the 13th century came to be known simply as the Hansa (Association). At the height of its success at the end of the 14th century, the Hansa encompassed 200 towns stretching from what is now the Netherlands to the Gulf of Finland. They traded eastwards into Russia, south to the Atlantic coasts of Spain and Portugal and as far west as Iceland.

The Hansa's rules stipulated that all trade with Shetland should be through their kontor (trading post) at Bergen in Norway. However, during the 15th century, the Hansa records begin to contain frequent references to individual merchants making illegal voyages to Shetland direct from Germany. In spite of the League imposing penalties such as confiscation of ships and goods and even expulsion from the Hansa, this clandestine trade grew and became even more blatant as the Hansa's control diminished. The accession of Shetland to Scotland from Norway in 1469 may have accelerated the process by weakening Shetland's link with Scandinavia.

The chief city of the Hanseatic League was Lübeck. A carved wooden replica of the city seal forms part of the exhibition in the Pier House (the Hamburg Böd) which was restored and opened as a museum of the trade in May 1986. The word "böd" comes from the German for storehouse, the meaning extended to encompass trading post. A cast of the Lübeck seal is mounted on the outside wall of the Pier House above the ground floor door. However, most of the merchants who came to Shetland were from Hamburg and Bremen. The earliest record of German merchants in Whalsay dates from 1557, although they had probably been trading there well before that date. The event recorded concerned a Bremen skipper called Kurt Hamelingk. Kurt's crew had been over at Laxfirth on the Shetland Mainland doing some business and arrived back late. For some reason, Kurt lost his temper and attacked them with a handspike. The crew defended themselves and the ship's carpenter, Gert Brecker, broke two of the skipper's fingers with a piece of wood. Two weeks later, Kurt died, unexpectedly. Some time afterwards, Kurt's brother arrived in Whalsay and accused the carpenter of murder. Brecker went into hiding but eventually hunger forced him to give himself up. He was taken back to Bremen to be tried but his fate is not recorded.

The earliest reference to the Germans having a building in Whalsay is in connection with an attack by pirates on another Bremen merchant called Herman Schroder in 1556. It is recorded that the pirates fired on his booth at Symbister and destroyed it. A document dated 1715 which was found among the Symbister House papers (the records of the Bruce family who were the lairds of Whalsay from the late 16th century until their bankruptcy in the 1920s) refers to two booths: the Bremen Booth at Symbister and another in Saltness. From the description of its

The Pier House.

The Bremen Böd.

The Hanseatic trade exhibition in the Pier House.

location in the document, the Bremen Booth seems to have been on the site of the large house which now stands at the head of the dock above the Pier House. The basement of the house may well have been the booth bombarded by the pirates who attacked Herman Schroder. The road leading past it and now called the Böd Walk used to be known as the Bremen Strasse.

The existence of a booth in Saltness ties in with local tradition. A large stone there, still called the Kurt Stane, is said to have been used as a pier by German ships and a shallow area in the adjacent bay called the North Voe is believed to have been created by ballast dumped by ships before loading cargo. In addition to Kurt Hemilingk, there are records of two other Kurts trading in Whalsay in 1640 – Kurt Lemkin and Kurt Warnekind. Any of them or perhaps some long-forgotten compatriot could have given his name to the stone. There is now no trace of the booth. A house built in the "ebb-stones" at Marrister is called the Böd, suggesting that it also may have been a base for German merchants.

This leaves the problem of the origin of the Pier House itself. The Whalsay antiquarian, R. Stewart Bruce, writing in the 1930s, believed that Hamburg merchants built it. They are first recorded in Whalsay in the early 17th century. The building stands with the sea on three sides at the end of a stone pier which encloses a small dock. The building and the dock were clearly built at the same time. The seaward end of the Pier House is shaped like the bow of a ship to deflect waves since the South Voe in which it stands has little shelter from certain wind directions.

The present building is on two floors, the upper storey being reached by an external stone stair. Whether it was originally built with two stories is uncertain as the upper gables seem to be made of the same granite as Symbister House, the laird's mansion built between 1820 and 1850 from stone brought across from Stavaness on the Shetland Mainland. A similar problem arises with the wooden wheel, built into the walls at eve level on the side facing the dock. Fitted with an ingenious system of ropes and pulleys, it was used to raise cargo from small boats in the dock as recently as the 1940s. The main reason why the Germans came to Whalsay was to buy the dried, salted ling and cod known as stockfish which was Shetland's chief export at the time. Whalsay is Shetland's main fishing community and still supplies fish to the continent – whitefish, herring, mackerel and shellfish. In the 1980s the local purse netters supplied herring and mackerel to ships congregating in Lerwick harbour each summer. These Klondykers, as they were called, were mainly from Eastern Bloc countries, chiefly Russia and Poland but there were also some from Lübeck, the former chief city of the Hanseatic League, so the German connection was continued in a modified form.

German merchants are known to have traded in more than 20 places in Shetland apart from Whalsay, in sheltered anchorages all-round the islands. The relatively even spread of their trading posts was no accident, for they were distributed by the Governor of Shetland under a licencing system so that each area of Shetland had access to one particular merchant or group of merchants. There were naturally disputes. Merchants would occasionally attempt to poach business from a neighbour and in such cases, the local courts would have to step in and adjudicate. A clue to the sheer number of merchants involved in the trade with Shetland comes from a commentary on a report by the governor on one particular dispute. The record quotes someone as saying that "there are more Hamburgers and Bremers around than frogs."

It is estimated that Shetland produced about ten per cent of the international supply of stockfish in the 16th century, the Germans carrying away about 500 tons of it each year. Dried fish was an important winter food as it was both highly nutritious and easily stored. The ling and cod were caught using hooks on long lines from small open boats called fourareens (four-oared boats) very similar in design to Viking vessels: most of these were imported from Norway in the 16th century. The fish were split open, salted and dried on shingle beaches. The technique was still being used in Shetland in the early 20th century. The stone huts or skeos where the fish were hung up at night or during rain can still be seen in Shetland. There is one in Whalsay on the beach near the Pier House. This beach was artificially created to dry fish, blocking off a small loch to the south, called Leebie's loch. The North Beach, in the North Voe, was similarly created, the sea formerly extending to the knoll known as Skibberhoull (Skipper's Hill).

The Germans brought in fishing gear – hooks, lines, ropes, tar and particularly important, the salt for curing the stock-fish. They also imported food and drink, for example, rye meal, wheat flour, bread, beer, and spirits; and household goods such as linen cloth, muslin, soap and ironmongery. Each year, the German traders sailed for Shetland in early spring, the voyage taking two or three weeks. Their ships were about the size of a modern fishing boat, perhaps 60 to 70 feet long with a crew of 6-18 – often consisting of relatives. They sailed for home in August or September.

The Germans had an ingenious way of keeping their customers. A merchant would give a year's credit on the understanding that the Shetlanders in his trading area would sell their goods to him alone the following year. The locals were thus kept in a state of permanent debt. In this way, as long as the Germans kept coming, there was little chance of a local merchant class emerging.

After the Germans left, the lairds carried on this system, which became known as the "truck system" which effectively enslaved tenants to the lairds, forcing them to fish for them to pay off debts. Towards the end of the 17th century, a combination of events signalled the end of the German trade with Shetland. Underlying these events was a current of feeling in Scotland that too much trade was in the hands of foreigners. This attitude was reflected in higher customs duties being placed on the German merchants and the appearance of some Scottish merchants in the Islands. The beginning of the end came with the French Wars which lasted from 1689 to 1713. French priva-teers repeatedly raided the islands and plundered the German merchants. Ten Shetland landowners who briefed the King's Council in 1696 reported that, "the German merchants are so broken and discouraged that it is to be feared that none of them will again return during the war." On top of this, the 1690s saw a series of cold summers resulting in poor crops and famine. The Shetlanders had less produce to trade with the Germans. Then, in 1700, there was a devastating outbreak of smallpox and hundreds of Shetlanders died.

In spite of these disasters, a few Germans kept coming. The final nails in the coffin were the Act of Union in 1707, which brought the English Navigation Laws into force in Scotland, forbidding the import of salt in foreign ships; and the Salt Tax of 1712. A letter from a Hamburg merchant, John Otto Bossau, to the Earl of Morton, provides a rather sad epitaph to the German trade with Shetland. Writing from Hamburg on the 5th October, 1712, he said: "I have been dealing to Shetland these 15 or 16 years and never had less than three or four ships loading from thence. I have trusted above £500 every year to the people. I paid all their duties for them and if they could pay me it was well; if not, I trusted them, which perhaps others won't do. And now I am turned out."

Downstairs in the Pier House there is an exhibition with figures in period costume and replicas of the goods traded, including the dried and salted ling and cod known as stockfish which was the main export from Shetland. Well-illustrated panels on both floors tell the story of the trade and Shetland's other Hanseatic ports. Two panels downstairs provide general information about Whalsay for visitors. The Pier House was restored and the museum is run by the Hanseatic Booth Restoration and Conservation Trust which was set up by the Shetland Islands Council in 1982.

Footnote: Neither Ian Tait, the Curator of the Shetland Museum, nor Brian Smith, the SIC's Archivist, believe that the Pier House is the Hamburg Böd and this view is backed up by research into the Hamburg merchants' activities in Shetland by a German professor. Their argument is that none of the Hanseatic böds were such substantial buildings as they were erected on relatively small plots of land leased from the lairds. The Pier House is clearly an integral part of the Hame Dock and even allowing for it being heightened using Stavaness granite at the time the Haa was being built, the lower part, built of local stone, would still have been a substantial building. Ian's theory is that it was built by the lairds in the 18th century when they took over the stockfish trade from the Germans. He cites the Lodberries in Lerwick and a similar structure of dock and Pier House at Busta House (the Pier House now demolished) as examples of similar developments from this period. Brian draws attention to an article written in the 1930s by R. Stuart Bruce, the laird's brother and well-known antiquarian, suggesting that the site of the Hamburg Böd may have been across the Böd Walk from the Bremen Böd on the site now occupied by JWJ's shop.

5

The Lairds

The Bruces of Symbister first obtained land on the island in 1572. The family originated in Fife and were descendants of Robert the Bruce's family. The first laird, William Bruce, came to Shetland in 1571 as clerk to his uncle Laurence Bruce of Cultmalindie who was governor of Shetland. Scotland had gained control of Shetland by default. In 1469 Shetland and Orkney had been pledged as surety against a wedding dowry being paid by the Norwegian King for his daughter who was to marry the King of Scotland. Since the dowry was never paid, the islands reverted to Scotland. Nothing much happened at first but in the 16th century, Scottish landed gentry started to move into the islands to take over.

William Bruce was foud to his uncle the governor, the equivalent of the procurator fiscal now, or prosecutor. In this role he accused the owner of the land at Symbister, Colbein Ormeston, of incest with one of his daughters and drove him off the island at sword point, seizing his land. At this time, land was held under Udal Law, the old Norse system and the land holders known as udallers or sometimes peerie lairds. These still existed in Whalsay at Marrister, Lee, West Linga and Challister. Scottish law now applied and successive lairds used their superior knowledge of this along with underhand tricks and clever intermarriages to eventually gain control of the rest of the island. Claus Hughson, the last laird of West Linga, was reputed to lose his land to the Bruces when, during a discussion on the possible transfer of the land, the laird dropped his pen. Claus picked it up and handed it to the laird, who claimed this constituted an intention to sign the sale document and marked Claus's X for him.

The last family on Linga, Jamiesons, left and went to Leith. A descendant of theirs, Leander Starr Jameson, (the spelling

The Auld Haa.

The Haa (Symbister House).

The last laird's wife's aunt being carried in a sedan chair.

Buildings around the Haa – Millhouse and the Bothies.

Leander Starr Jameson's information panel.

Leander Starr Jameson's grave.

corresponds with how the Whalsay Jamiesons pronounce their name) was the infamous leader of the Jameson Raid in South Africa which eventually precipitated the Boer War. Many Boers (descendants of the original Dutch settlers) had left Cape Province which was ruled by the British in the 1830s in the Great Trek and set up their own independent republics in the Orange Free State and Transvaal. In 1884 gold was discovered in the Witvatersrand (Johannesburg) and a gold rush ensued with miners (mainly British) flocking into the area and soon outnumbering the local Boers. After discriminatory legislation by the Transvaal against these "Uitlanders" (foreigners) they were on the verge of rebellion. Cecil Rhodes, the Governor of Cape Province, conceived a plan to precipitate this and take over the Transvaal with its rich goldfield for Britain. Jameson was to lead a column of 600 heavily armed men, including artillery pieces, from the British colony of Matabeleland to the north of Transvaal and join up with the revolting Uitlanders. However, the rebellion never materialised, and Jameson surrendered. He was tried in Britain and jailed but became something of a folk hero as the Germans had supported the Transvaal and anti-German feeling, which eventually culminated in the First World War, was strong. Jameson was exonerated and later became Prime Minister of the Cape Colony. A greener

Buildings around the Haa – the Heritage Centre.

area of land in the centre of West Linga shows where a former croft has been. The Laird of Lee was accused of concealing that he had found a cask of gin or rum and threatened with imprisonment unless he handed over his land. The Laird of Challister was told that if he handed over his land, he "would always eat at the Laird's table." There was a traditional old Norse custom known as "opgestry" whereby an elderly person could make their land over to someone who undertook to look after them for the remainder of their life. In this case, after the Laird of Challister signed over his land to Bruce, he was sent a "fine table". The Marrister estate fell into the Bruce's hands in 1836 through marriage into the Peerie Laird's family. Eventually, the whole island was under their control.

The Bruce's first home on the island, the Auld Haa, was built in 1702 by Laird John Bruce at the top of the Böd Walk leading uphill from the Pier House. It is now a private dwelling house. In 1820, the sixth laird, Robert Bruce, started building a new Georgian mansion for the family, now called the Haa or Symbister House. Not completed until nearly 30 years later (Robert Bruce who died in 1844 never lived in it) the astronomical cost in these days of £30,000 eventually bankrupted the family in the 1920s. The Haa was built in granite quarried at Stavaness on the Mainland and shipped across Linga Sound. The stone was hoisted ashore using the wheel and pulley system set into the wall of the Pier House. The laird's schooner, *Margaret*, was wrecked in a storm at Stavaness in 1825, no doubt contributing to the delay in completing the building.

The finished article had 22 rooms. Behind it to the east was an enclosed courtyard from which a tower rose housing the long drop toilet accessed by two stone staircases with a dove cote above it. When the Haa became derelict this courtyard was the scene of clandestine football matches on Sunday afternoons in the early 1960s. At that time the Sabbath was still considered holy and such activities were frowned on. Beyond this courtyard, another one aptly called the Midden Court was lined with buildings housing cattle and pigs. An outer strip of buildings enclosed both these courtyards housing stables, a smithy and the millhouse, where corn was ground using water from the Mill Loch just to the east. The mill continued in operation until the 1940s. Access through these buildings to the road outside was through two archways. In the middle of the strip was a belfry, the bell used to summon farm workers to meals. The local heritage centre is now located in part of this outer strip of buildings and there is a long-range plan to rehabilitate the whole complex. The Haa fell vacant shortly after the last laird, William Bruce, died in 1944 and gradually fell into dereliction – a fertile playground for local children looking for the bullet hole in the wall where a visitor had shot himself in the 1920s. In 1964, the Haa was converted into a school centralising all education on the island.

In 1863, the second last laird, Robert Bruce, set up a farm in the central part of the island, recorded as covering 800 acres in 1871 of which 100 acres were arable. It extended from Harlsdale to the boundary of the crofts at Hamister and as far east as Livister. Traces of cultivated rigs (fields) can still be seen between the croft at Livister and the Livister Loch. A strip of four cottages were built just west of and across the road from the Auld Haa to house farm workers, who were mostly brought in from the Scottish Mainland. Another strip of cottages for workers known as the Bothies was built just to the south-east of the Haa itself. Two shepherds' cottages were built at Whitefield. The central scattald, now known as the Fence, was taken off the crofters and added to the farm, a source of much discontent as voiced to an Inquiry in 1889 by the newly formed Crofters Commission set up to hear grievances and fix fair rents after the Crofters Act of 1886 which gave crofters security of tenure. There had originally been three scattalds on the island, one known as the Clate Hill serving Clate, Sandwick and Huxter, the Fence in the centre of the island and the Auld Hill, serving crofts from Hamister north on the west side and Traewick and Isbister on the east side.

In 1903, the farm was broken up into 28 crofts and the Fence scattald returned to the crofters, each with a 28th share in it. The new crofts were in Harlsdale, Symbister, Saltness and along the south side of the central valley from Skibberhoull to Whitefield. Robert Bruce was something of a tyrant. He banished a family living in the Hammars, down near the sea to the east of Huxter, from the island for failing to keep up with their rent and confiscated their cow in compensation for the lost rent. Seeing the land now, steep and rocky and obviously an outset from Huxter where some previous tenant had been forced off better land, it's hardly surprising that they struggled with their rent.

The story is that two Anderson men from Sandwick, cousins Lang Robbie and Short Robbie, smuggled the family's cow across Linga Sound to Nesting where they had found somewhere to live. The laird found out about this and banished the men from the island and they were never heard off again. An alternative version of this story is that the same two men helped a Robertson man from Whitefield to lift his cow over the gate at Sudheim (Sodom), the Sodom Grind, just below the present day Saeter housing scheme, after he had been exiled and was determined to take his cow with him. The problem with this version of the story is that the Whitefield crofts weren't formed until after the farm was broken up in 1903. Whichever story is true, Lang Robbie Anderson certainly was expelled from the island in 1868, leaving his girl-friend, Margaret Jardine, pregnant with the author's grandfather.

The same laird expelled two Vatshoull men who had gone to the Greenland whaling against the laird's rules prohibiting this as he wanted all the men to stay on the island and fish for him. The men's mother walked the length of the island to the Haa to plead their cause with the laird to no avail. She is then said to have laid a curse on the laird, saying that there would come a day when there would be no Bruces left in Whalsay, that their great mansion house would stand empty and derelict with the grass growing up between the flagstones and the local children would play freely in the grounds and courtyards. With the death of the last laird in 1944, the subsequent dereliction of the Haa and its later resurrection as the school, her prophesy appears to have been fulfilled.

In line with his personality, Robert Bruce was not known for his standards of personal hygiene. He was reputed to be infested with lice, which lived in a pocket of skin at his shoulder blades. When he died and was being carried in his coffin to the kirkyard, the story is that lice could be seen crawling out from under the coffin lid.

6

The Fishing Industry

Commercial fishing started in Whalsay as far back as the 13th century with the coming of the Hanseatic merchants. Fishing from fourareens, using baited long lines in waters up to 10 miles offshore, cod and ling were caught, split, salted and dried on the beaches artificially created on the South and North Voes of Symbister.

When the Germans were forced out in the early 18th century, the lairds moved into the vacuum, financing the Haaf fishing era by purchasing the larger sixareens from Norway and pioneering markets on the British Mainland, Spain and Portugal. The infamous truck system developed whereby tenants were indebted to the laird for the cost of their boats and gear and their living costs, paying off what they could from the year's earnings but never getting into credit, so they were forced to go on fishing for him.

The haaf fishing grounds were a long way offshore, up to 50 miles on the west side of Shetland towards the edge of the continental shelf, where they talked of "rowing Foula doon". There were no navigation aids, other than the sun and stars and birds and the run of the sea known as the "moder dy", which was essentially the reflection or rebound of the sea off land regardless of the wind direction. The Polynesians used similar methods in their Pacific voyages. The species caught were cod, ling and tusk and processing methods the same as in Hanseatic times. During the haaf season, from around the 20th May to Lammas in mid-August, stations were set up in remote areas nearer the fishing grounds in order to save time getting to them. In Whalsay's case this was on Grif Skerry, one of the chain of small islands lying east of the island. Living conditions were primitive, the shelters drystone built with pones (turf) for roofs and a raised area at one end for sleeping. Fish were landed and split on the neighbouring East Linga and then shipped to Symbister for salting and drying. Haaf fishing was incredibly dangerous. Although the open sixareens were extremely good sea boats, if caught at sea a long way from shore in storms, accidents were inevitable. A number of such fishing disasters occurred in the 19th century and eventually brought the Haaf fishery to a close towards the end of the century. The last Whalsay sixareen was hauled into its noost in 1885.

The worst disaster occurred in 1832 when a sudden July storm caught the fleet at sea. Around 20 sixareens were lost from throughout Shetland and 111 men. Some boats were driven to the coast of Norway, other crews were picked up by Dutch herring buses. Four Whalsay boats and 19 men were lost. The crew of one boat, skippered by Tammas Hughson, was picked up by an American barque heading for Philadelphia. They spent nearly six months there before getting a passage back home. The story goes that when they landed at Sandwick the skipper's dog took off from Brough in a state of excitement to meet them. Another version goes that the dog belonged to another crew member, Alexander Anderson - Wharry Daa - and that he landed just below his house at Marrister. Whichever version is true, it seems that in these days of poor communications, a dog knew that the men were alive before any of his two-legged friends. On 20/21st July, 1881, the Gloup Disaster

The sixareen Vaila Mae under sail in Lerwick Harbour.

The Research.

The Tranquillity, *a modern whitefish boat.*

Serene, a purse netter launched in 2018.

was virtually the death knell of the haaf fishing. Ten Yell boats and 58 men were lost in a sudden storm and many boats and men from Delting were also lost.

After the sixareen era had ended, long line fishing continued from the smaller fourareens and was pursued in winter as well as summer. And disasters continued to dog it. In December 1887 part of the Whalsay fleet were at sea when a sudden storm blew up. The morning had been fine but there was a blue tinge to the sky and a heavy swell running in the sea, suggesting bad weather further offshore. Most of the boat crews from the south end of the island were suspicious of the weather and stayed ashore. Two Brough crews had just had new boats built and were anxious to start paying them off. They decided to chance their luck and others from the north end followed their example. The wind came

up suddenly from the north, accompanied by a blinding blizzard. Boats cut their lines away and started rowing for their lives. One boat, skippered by James Williamson, drove ashore at Ericru, not far from their home beach, although they had no idea where they were. One crew man, Andrew Williamson, the author's grandfather, managed to jump ashore but the boat capsized on two others. In a feat of superhuman strength, the skipper managed to lift the boat off them and drag them ashore. One of them, Peter Gilbertson, was badly injured. One boat with two brothers of Andrew Williamson disappeared completely. A woman who was reputed to have second sight claimed that she had had a vision of them foundering on the Soldian Baa. Another boat, skippered by Laurence Moar, made it to Lerwick but by the time they got there two of the crew, Andrew and Laurence Anderson from the Burns, were dead from exhaustion and exposure. The third crewman was unconscious. The skipper had raised the sail and steering with one hand and bailing with the other had managed to reach Lerwick. Another boat came ashore in Bressay with one man, James Arthur, dead from exposure. In all from the eight boats and 32 men fishing that day, seven men lost their lives. The two Anderson men from the Burns who were lost were the father and uncle of Andrew Williamson's future wife, Mary (the author's grandmother). She went on to live to nearly 101.

Before the haaf fishing era ended in 1885, half-decked and fully decked boats had been appearing, offering more comfort and safety to their crews. In 1892 the first smack rigged vessel was fitted out for a Sandwick (South Mainland) crew, marking the start of the sailboat era. In 1900, the *Swan*, the largest boat ever built in Shetland with a 67 foot keel and 20 feet beam, was launched. In 1908 she was fitted out in smack rig. She fished until the mid-1950s when she was sold to the British Mainland and eventually fell into disrepair until Tammy Moncrieff from Lerwick rescued her. A trust was set up to rehabilitate her, which was completed in 1991 and she is now preserved as an example of a boat of the sail fishing era and used for training and tourist purposes.

The 1890s saw the start of the herring fishery. Up until then, local people had not exploited the herring stocks around the islands.

Mackerel had been caught inshore as bait for the line fishing but for centuries herring had been the preserve of Dutch fishermen who came in their booms and buses each year in June and stayed till August. In the 17th century as many as 20,000 Dutch fishermen would congregate in Bressay Sound, leading to the development of Lerwick as the Shetland capital, replacing Scalloway with the tyrant Earl Patrick Stewart's castle.

Herring were fished using drift nets at night. In 1878, only around 1,000 crans of herring were landed in Shetland. By 1884 there were 900 boats at the herring fishing and the following year 370,000 crans were landed. The herring boom had started. In 1922, a herring curing station was opened at Symbister by J&M Shearer, brothers Arthur and Magnus and their uncle James (known as Buckfit) from Bells Brae House. They took over from Hay & Company who had barrelled herring there for some time. Gutters huts were erected for the girls from the north end of the island so that they could get to work early. Barrels were made, which continued into the early 1960s, when Attie Williamson used to turn out seven a day. When a big catch was landed, older women, known as the "Overly" women were called in to help out with the gutting. In the 1920s, the station cured 3,500 to 4,500 crans a season. A kippering kiln had been set up by Hay & Company in the 1880s and this continued under J&M Shearer. The market for the herring after the First World War was mainly Spain and Portugal as traditional markets for fish in Russia and Germany had been disrupted by the war and the Russian Revolution.

The whitefish industry had continued after the haaf era using half-decked and decked boats, now a winter rather than a summer fishing and not so far offshore. In the first decade of the 1900s, haddock lines were replacing the long lines for ling and cod. Haddock line boats like the *Venture* and the *Dilligent* were just around 20 to 30 feet in keel length. Mechanisation was appearing, the first steam capstan being installed on the *Maid of Thule* (Buckfit's boat) in 1896. (She was converted to steam in the early 1920s.) In 1909, the first petrol/paraffin engine appeared. Lines were baited at home by the women, using mainly imported mussels and salted mackerel. Each crew member had two or three lines. The fish were preserved in ice recovered from frozen lochs and ponds and stored in ice houses insulated with "feals" (turf). The fish that was landed at Symbister was stored in the Fish House to be shipped out on the *Earl of Zetland*.

In 1915 there were 15 boats operating from Whalsay, all but two the drifters known as Fifies with a keel length of around 50 to 70 feet. One of the exceptions was the *Gracie Brown* which was a carvel-built Zulu. She was motorized in the 1920s and the last of her class operating in 1937. By 1930, boats were beginning to be motorized. In 1928 there were still 13 large sail boats; only two survived by 1936. The *Swan* was fitted with a Gardner engine in 1935.

The Second World War again virtually put an end to commercial fishing for the duration of the war. Four small boats soldiered on, the *Fern, Eclipse, Venture* and *Olive*, all under 40 feet in length, at the haddock line in winter and herring in summer. It was slow to pick up again after 1945 as money was scarce. Second hand dual-purpose boats around 60 to 70 feet keel were bought from Mainland Scotland fishing for whitefish in winter and herring in summer. The fleet gradually built up with boats like the *Fair Dawn, Liberty* and *Mary Jane*. The *Bonnie Isle* was new built in Scalloway in 1949 for skipper Willie Polson. Seine netting for whitefish now became the order of the day. It had been experimented with just before and during the war (the *Ocean's Gift* being a notable pioneer) and now became the preferred technique. Boats were anchored off in both the North and South Voes, men rowing off to them in foureens. The old pier at Symbister, below where the boating club is now, was destroyed in a gale in 1953 and not replaced with a new one extending out westwards from the end of the West or New Dock for a few years. Fishing was rather in the doldrums in the early to mid-1950s and a lot of men came ashore to work at the Whalsay water scheme, the installation of the radar system at Saxavord in Unst and then the Skerries water scheme. A revival started in 1955 with the building of the first *Serene* by Mackie and Dodie Polson and Willie Anderson from Hamister. With the state of the fishing at the time and the cost of a brand-new boat, (£13,000, a lot of money at that time) people thought they were mad. But they paid off their debt in one season and others followed their example (aided by a government loan and grant scheme) and purchased new boats – including the *Orion, Zephyr, Unity* and *Planet,* all arriving before the end of the decade. The 1960s saw a boom in both the herring and white fisheries and money flowed into the island. J&M Shearer closed their herring station in 1962, consolidating their business at their station at Garthspool in Lerwick which continued in operation until 1977.

During the 1960s, large Norwegian purse netters began appearing in Shetland waters catching herring and mackerel in huge quantities. Inevitably, local fishermen saw an opportunity here and again it was the *Serene,* skippered by Mackie Polson, which led the way, their new purser arriving in 1969. She was joined by another six in the next few years. However, this vastly increased catching capacity by both local and foreign vessels had a drastic effect on herring stocks. Catches by the drift net fleet plummeted and one by one they gave up. In 1968 the *Research,* the last of the old originally sail-powered Zulu drifters, with her legendary skipper Bobby Polson, Mackie's father, finally threw in the towel. Drift net herring fishing came to an end in 1975 when the last boat, the *Replenish* from Burra Isle gave up mid-season, having caught very little. In 1973, Britain joined the Common Market and with regulation becoming the order of the day, herring fishing in the British sector of the North Sea was banned in 1977. This created serious problems for the purse net fleet. They adjusted by starting to fish for herring in the Minch, which wasn't affected by the North Sea ban, but in 1978 herring fishing was banned there too, again because of depletion of the stocks. Attention then switched to fishing for mackerel in South-West England out of Falmouth, which was not popular with the locals. In 1977, the European Union extended its fisheries limits to 200 miles so East European vessels could no longer fish for mackerel off the west and south-west coasts of the UK. This provided an opportunity for the local pursers to fish for Eastern Block klondykers (factory ships) which would congregate in Ullapool in August for the Minch mackerel season and then Falmouth at the end of October for the South-West England season. To fill the gap between the Cornwall fishery and the Minch season, some boats trawled for whitefish in the remaining winter months. Others tried diversifying into horse mackerel and blue whitings. Finally, in 1983, the North Sea herring fishing was re-opened, the stocks having recovered and klondykers now started to assemble in Lerwick buying both herring and mackerel. Fishing was now heavily regulated to preserve stocks with quotas for each species and in the case of whitefish a policy to reduce the fleet size which lead to decommissioning of some boats. Around 1990, pelagic trawling, initially pair-trawling, came in to replace the purse net system. On the whitefish front, in the mid-1960s there was a change-over from seine net to trawling. Currently in 2019 the Whalsay fishing fleet consists of seven pelagic trawlers from 70 to 80 metres in length (the new serene is 82 metres) able to carry 2,000 tons of fish (the newer ones 3,000) These boats now cost between £25 and £30 million to build; seven whitefish trawlers from 15 to 30 metres in length and able to carry 1,000 boxes of fish; and four scallop boats. Other smaller boats are at the lobster and crab fishing. Salmon is farmed in cages in the North Voe. There is no mussel farming which elsewhere in Shetland is a major export earner.

In 1970, John Tait, a former maths teacher, married to a Whalsay girl, opened a fish factory in the disused Brough School. He built a new factory at Symbister in 1977. At its peak employing around 80 people, processing whitefish and latterly salmon, this was a valuable contributor to employment in Whalsay especially for women. Its closure in 2011, mainly due to transport costs and congestion on the ferries, was a major blow to the island. Bearing in mind that fishing is one of the most dangerous occupations, with 179 fatalities in the UK between 2000 and 2014AD, Whalsay has had surprisingly few fishing related deaths since the days of the open boats. In April 1881, John Jamieson from Sandwick was drowned saving a crewmate, Geordie Anderson, who had gone overboard from the smack *Eagle*, one of the earliest decked boats at a time when the haaf fishing was coming to an end. Geordie was saved but John did not survive his heroic effort. A Skaw fourareen mysteriously disappeared in calm weather on New Year's Day 1891 with the loss of four men: Arthur Johnson; brothers Robert and Edward Bruce; and Laurence Simpson. Auld Tammie Bruce, a neighbour, who was believed to have second sight, saw them going off when he was coming ashore and appears to have had a premonition about it. Jamie a Hoose (Hutchison) was drowned off the sailboat *Valkyrie* in July 1935 at the age of 36 when he was knocked overboard by the jib while trying to lower the sail. His crewmate, Glybbie's Johnnie (son of Auld Glybbie) went in to rescue him with a lifeline and the crew managed to get them back on board but Jamie had already died. Johnnie was awarded a medal for his valiant effort. In March 1969, Willie a Skaw (Hutchison) was lost off the *Brighter Morn*, caught up in their scallop dredge. He was only 21. Christopher Robertson, Grunnataing, was drowned in April 1992, aged 40, when he was fishing alone for lobsters off Isbister. Most recently, in October 2010, Alan Douglas Arthur of Saltness drowned, again at the lobsters, when he became entangled in a creel rope and dragged down.

7

Agriculture and Peat Cutting

Traditional crofting continued much as it had done for centuries until the 1960s. The 1883 Napier Commission (Royal Commission into the Condition of Crofters and Cottars in the Highlands and Islands) highlighted the problem of insecurity of tenure which was rectified in the Crofters Act of 1886. An 1889 inquiry by the Crofter's Commission, set up by the 1886 Act, into grievances and to fix fair rents, made further improvements in the conditions of crofters. Earlier, in 1871, the Truck Commission (semi-serfdom in the Shetland Isles. Report of the Royal Commission into the Truck System, 1871) had effectively ended the system, originally developed by the Hanseatic merchants and adopted by the lairds, whereby men were effectively forced to remain fishing for them by advancing them credit which in practice could never be fully paid off.

In Whalsay, crofts were generally around seven or eight acres in size, with a share in the scattald where sheep could be grazed and cattle tethered during the summer. There were three scattalds, one serving Clate, Sandwick and Huxter known as the Clate Hill; the Fence, serving the 28 crofts formed from the breakup of the laird's farm; and the Auld Hill, serving the rest of the island.

Crofting activities followed an annual rhythm according to the seasons, planting in the "voar" (spring) weeding and hay cutting in the summer and harvesting in the "hairst" (autumn). The main crop was oats, mainly Shetland oats, although barley had been introduced by the first Neolithic settlers. Potatoes had been introduced around 1730 and became the staple diet (boiled fish and tatties with melted fat or butter). Potatoes originated in South America and had been introduced to Britain during the reign of Elizabeth I. They thrived in Shetland's climate. Kale had been grown at least since the 17th century, plantie crub building to rear young

Delling (digging) with Shetland spades at Whitefield – Robbie John Anderson, Mary and Peter Hughson - the Author's brother and sister. The house (now modernized) in the background, is where the Author was born. This is believed to be the last time that a traditional three-person team delled in Whalsay.

Building a scroo (corn stack) of Shetland oats.

*Family
gathering
waar
(seaweed) for
fertilizer at
Boatshoose.*

*Willie
and Ruby
Hutchison
maain'
(mowing)
corn (oats).*

*Rooin'
(shearing)
sheep.*

*Man castin'
(cutting)
peats with a
tushker.*

plants from seed resulting in the destruction of many Neolithic houses. Kathleen Stewart (nee Simpson) from Houll, tells that her father Sandy, who was born in 1900, could remember crubs being built from Neolithic houses at the Houll Loch. Plantie crubs are a prominent feature in the landscape in some parts of the island. Dry-stone built and mostly circular in design, although there are some rectangular ones, they are generally about four and a half feet high and six to eight feet in diameter, with no doorway – some had flat stones protruding halfway up to act as a stile for clambering in and out. They are always found in the scattald, often near lochs. Ian Tait, in his book Shetland Vernacular Buildings explains that poorer scattald land was used to hinder vigorous growth of the seedlings so that they developed strong roots but little foliage which helped transplanting in kale yards in the in-bye land on crofts. Turnips (neeps) were a later addition to the staple crops, a yard in the Brough area known as the Neapy Yard believed to be where they were first grown on the island. Grass was cut for hay for winter feeding for livestock.

In the early voar, the byres and hen houses were mucked out and the muck wheeled out in wheelbarrows to the rigs (fields). Seaweed (waar) was gathered from the beaches and spread on the land as fertiliser. In some place's sheep grazed on seaweed in the "ebb-stanes": this can still be seen below the Böd at Marrister, where they occasionally get marooned on a skerry. The land was prepared for planting by "delling" (digging) with the traditional Shetland spade, usually with teams of three people working together. The "rigs" for oats were then harrowed using rectangular wooden structures with protruding metal spikes prior to the seeds being sown. During the summer the tattie rigs were "howed" (hoed) to get rid of weeds such as "arva" and then "heaped", the earth being scraped up against the tattie "shows" (foliage). In the hairst the oats were "shared" (cut), the women using "corn heuks" (sickles), the men scythes. Bundles of corn stalks were then gathered together, a band made from a few stalks wound around the middle of the bunch and knotted to form a sheave, four of which were then leant against each other to dry. When they were dry, they were "hirded" (carried) to near the croft steadings where they were built into "scroos" (stacks). Grass was "maaed" (mowed) using scythes, then spread out and turned over several times with rakes until it was dry enough to "cole" (small conical piles of hay) and finally hird to where the hay "dess" (stack) was built up beside the scroos of corn.

As regards livestock, most crofts could support two "kye" (cattle) and a calf and 20 to 30 sheep which were kept in the scattald. The kye spent most of the winter indoors in the byre, fed on hay, oats and kale. Most crofts also had a pig, kept in a sty. The pig and some sheep were slaughtered in the hairst to provide food over the winter. The author recalls a macabre pantomime enacted when he was a boy when a pig being killed by his father escaped and ran around in circles for a while, blood spurting from its neck, until it collapsed and died. This was a bit of a disaster as the blood was used to make "bloody puddings" (black puddings). Some of the mutton was "reestit", hung up to dry on the "rip" (a clothesline also used to dry washing) in the smoke above the open fire. Reestit mutton soup was considered to be a delicacy. Hens were kept for eggs and older ones eaten when they had passed their lay-by date. The communal bull was kept by Alec Barclay in the 1950s. People from all over the island had to lead their cows when they were "riding" (seeking calf) to the Burns, where Alec lived, for servicing by the bull. During the summer, the sheep in the scattalds were "caaed" (chased) to the crue (corral) for rooing (shearing) and dipping to get rid of "keds" (ticks). This tended to be a major social occasion. Although some crofts had horses, sometimes used for ploughing and harrowing, there was no tradition of keeping Shetland ponies on Whalsay as was the case in Unst for example.

Traditionally, barns and byres were attached to the gables of the croft houses as they had been in Viking times. In the Western Isles, this style of building was known as a Longhouse. When the laird built his "model villages" at Brough, Sandwick, Clate and Challister this style was retained. Toilets were often ramshackle buildings attached to the byre or barn. Flushing toilets were not available until after a piped water supply was provided in 1953. Before that water was carried from wells, most crofts having their own well.

Peats for fuel were "casted" (cut) in April, using a "tushker", a tool unique to Shetland which allowed the peat to be lifted onto the back of the peat bank and built into a dyke. The surface turf was first removed using a "ripper" (resembling a tushker but with a straight blade). The peat was up to three feet deep allowing three peats to be cut vertically, the upper, "mossy", one being called the "styumpie", the "third peat" being top quality, drying to form "blue clods". As the peats dried off in the dykes, they were "raised" into small piles of peats set on end called "raisings" and then built into bigger "roogs" when they were completely dry. Traditionally they were carried home in "kyshies" (straw baskets) by the women and built up into peat stacks outside the houses. Sometimes they were left in the peat hill and carried home as required. This was known as "Dyaan ta stack". By the 1960s this task was being performed by tractors with trailers.

From the 1960s traditional crofting started dying out fairly rapidly, most crofts just converted to grazing sheep. Many apportionments were railed in and re-seeded for sheep grazing from the scattald with grants from the Crofters Commission. Cultivation all but disappeared apart from some tatties and kale. Hay was cut using motor mowers and silage made rather than hay, blue barrels from the Sullom Voe Oil terminal often being used to store it. Peat casting has also all but died out, to be replaced by electricity, gas and oil for cooking and heating. The scars of peat banks remain prominent in the landscape as a reminder of a world now gone.

8

World Wars

Both World Wars, the first from 1914–18 and the second from 1939–45, had a substantial impact on Whalsay. Many men were in the Royal Naval Reserve (RNR) and were called up to the navy while many others were in the merchant navy. Others volunteered or were called up into the services. In the Second World War there was a military base on the island using the new radar technology to monitor ship and aircraft movements around the islands. Economic life, especially the fishing industry, was seriously disrupted.

In the First World War, 183 local men went to war and 24 died. The roll of honour can be seen on the memorial in the kirk yard at Kirkaness. The majority of the deaths were at sea but there were others on land on the Western Front. Four Whalsay men were lost off the navy ship HMS *Ramsey* on 8th August, 1915, and another two saved. In the First World War, the practice was to group men from the same area together both in ships and army units. Joseph Kay from Zoar was killed at the Battle of Jutland on 31st May, 1916, when the Dreadnought battleship HMS *Malaya* was sunk. On land, William Arthur from Sudheim (erroneously spelled Sodom on the Ordnance Survey maps), a company sergeant-major, was killed in action on the Western Front in September 1918, just two months before the war ended. Gilbert Arthur from Brough was wounded at Ypres on the Western Front also in 1918. He died in hospital in Aberdeen the following year from the after-effects of his wounds. The laird's cousin, Lieutenant William McCrae Bruce, won a posthumous VC for his actions defending a trench captured from the Germans at the battle for the town of Givenchy in France.

Others survived. Robert Williamson from Brough (a son of Mary Williamson) signed up in 1914 at the age of 18 and served throughout the war on the Western Front with the Cameronians, 10th Scottish Rifles. His battalion were involved in the earliest battle where

All that remains of the hospital where Lowrie Jamieson convalesced in Madagascar after his ordeal.

The beautiful old French colonial style hospital was so badly damaged in a cyclone in 1972 that it was abandoned.

First World War memorial.

Second World War memorial.

1939 – 45 WAR

ROBERT ARTHUR, BROUGH, O. M. M.N., SS CALDARE, 13TH MAY 1942, AGE 43
ROBERT J. BRUCE, TREAWICK, BOSUN M.N., SS CIRALDA, 30TH JAN. 1940, AGE 34
THOMAS BRUCE, SKAW, A.B. M.N., SS FIRCREST, 25TH AUG. 1940, AGE 19
PETER J. GILBERTSON, BROUGH, A.B. M.N., SS MILL END, 19TH JAN. 1940, AGE 42
CHARLES HUTCHISON, BROUGH, A.B. M.N., SS SOURABAYA, 27TH OCT. 1942, AGE 30
GEORGE IRVINE, BOOTH PARK, A. B. M.N., SS EMPIRE HERITAGE, 17TH OCT. 1944, FROM WAR INJURY, AGE 62
ROBERT L. IRVINE, ISBISTER, PRIVATE 2ND GORDON HIGHLANDERS, 5TH AUG. 1945, AGE 24
WILLIAM A. IRVINE, KNOWE & EDINBURGH, A.B. M.N., SS ROYAL FUSILIER, 1942, AGE 43
MAGNUS A. JAMIESON, SANDWICK, A.B. M.N., 13TH NOV. 1942, AGE 22
THOMAS G. LEASK, SERG. BOSUN M.N., SS PHILIPP M., 24TH FEB. 1944, AGE 39
THOMAS G. LEASK, ISBISTER & LEITH, SEC. OFFICER, M.N., SS BRITISH COLONY, 13TH MAY 1942, AGE 38
JAMES MAINLAND, SYMBISTER & LEITH, A.B. M.N., SS CRICHTOUN, 18TH MARCH 1945, AGE 50
ARTHUR B. POLESON, MYRTLE COTTAGE, CARPENTER M.N., SS SOURABAYA, 27TH OCT. 1942, AGE 29
ROBERT J. POLESON, TRIPWELL, O.M. R.N., H.M.S. RAWALPINDI, 23RD NOV. 1939, AGE 25
THOMAS B. ROBERTSON, SKAW, L. CPL. R. ARMOURED CORPS, 21ST OCT. 1944, AGE 25
ROBERT J. SHEARER, SKAW, A.E. M.N., 23RD AUG. 1942, AGE 31
JAMES SIMPSON, HOULL, A.B. M.N., SS PERINGTON COURT, 5TH OCT. 1942, AGE 36
THOMAS H. SIMPSON, LUNDA, SEAMAN R.N., FROM WAR INJURY 8TH JAN. 1947, AGE 22
GILBERT STEWART, HILLHEAD, O.M. M.N., SS CRICHTOUN, 18TH MARCH 1945, AGE 55
MAGNUS STEWART, BROULL, SEC. OFFICER, M.N., SS SINJKISHNA, 24TH FEB. 1941, AGE 31
JAMES J. WILLIAMSON, ISBISTER, BOSUN M.N., SS CRICHTOUN, 18TH MARCH 1945, AGE 35
THOMAS WILLIAMSON, HARRISTER, A.B. M.N., SS CIRALDA, 30TH JAN. 1940, AGE 54

*Major Robbie
Williamson,
son of Mary
Williamson.*

Second World War military camp at Harlsdale.

Lowrie Jamieson who spent 17 days on a lifeboat in the Indian Ocean after his ship was torpedoed.

Willie Anderson and Andrew Sandison who survived their ships being torpedoed in the Second World War.

Second World War military buildings on Wart of Clate.

poison gas was used by the British at Loos in September, 1915 and the following year held the trenches in a salient sticking out from the main front line and overlooked by the Germans called The Kink, described in the regiment's war records as "among the worst British positions of the Western Front." They later took part in the Battle of the Somme in 1916, some of the bloodiest fighting in the whole war. Robbie emerged as a regimental sergeant major. He joined up again for the second war as a commissioned officer and rose to the rank of Major in the Black Watch, latterly commanding an Italian prisoner of war camp in the Scottish Highlands. Willie Anderson, from Whitefield, served on a hospital ship at the Battle of Jutland and in the Second World War was at the D-Day landings. Bobby Bruce, originally from Skaw but living at Brough after he married, was in the navy at Gallipoli. He famously obtained a pair of boots off a dead Turkish soldier: according to his story he got the first boot off alright but was having difficulty with the second one when he came under fire and had to saw off the leg above the boot with his bayonet to get the pair. He was renowned for his tall tales so this may have been apocryphal.

The death toll in Second World War was remarkably similar to First World War, with 22 names on the war memorial in the Kirk yard. The Roll of Service has 154 names including several women. Again, there were some multiple deaths from the same incident. For example, just weeks before the war ended, the merchant ship the SS *Crightoun* was sunk off Lowestoft by a German motor torpedo boat (MTB), operating out of the occupied Channel Islands, with the loss of three Whalsay men: Jamie Williamson from Grunna- taing (another son of Mary Williamson); Gilbert Stewart from the Hillhead; and James Mainland from Symbister. Jamie left four sons, the eldest just eight years old. Two men, Robert John Bruce from Traewick, who left four daughters and Thomas Williamson from Houll were lost off the SS *Giralda* when she was sunk by enemy aircraft off South Ronaldsay in Orkney in January 1940. Two more, Arthur Poleson from Isbister and Charles Hutchison from Houll, were lost when the SS *Sourabaya* was torpedoed in 1942. Robert James Poleson, Tripwell, Quartermaster on the navy ship *Rawalpindi*, died when she was sunk by the German Destroyer, *Scharnhorst*, south east of Iceland. Robert Irvine from Isbister, a private in the Gordon Highlanders, was taken prisoner at the fall of Singapore in 1942 and died from cholera in Thailand the following year doing forced labour for the Japanese on the Burma Railway. A number of men were involved in the D-Day landings in Normandy in June 1944. George Stewart, Hillhead, was mentioned in dispatches for distinguished service when he went under fire to survey Omaha Beach in Normandy for siting of the Mulberry Harbours prior to the Americans landing. Samuel Irvine, Challister, was at the beaches the night before the landings clearing mines. Angus Williamson from the Old Manse landed with the Marines, surviving his landing craft being sunk.

Several men had harrowing experiences after their ships were torpedoed. Willie Anderson, Clate, spent 16 days on a life raft in the Atlantic off West Africa before being rescued. His ship, the *Rio Azul* had loaded iron ore in Freetown, Liberia, and left for Britain in a convoy. They soon came under attack from a submarine pack and ships started going down all around them. The convoy had to disperse, and they were left on their own. Willie was in his cabin ironing a shirt when a torpedo hit them amidships, breaking her in two. He grabbed his lifejacket and ran up on deck. One of the lifeboats had been smashed and rather than head for the other one he decided to rely on the life rafts floating free and jumped into the water. As the ship went down, both bow and stern pointing skywards, he spotted a life raft some distance away. While he was swimming towards it, the submarine surfaced ahead of him and shouted to the men on the raft and then quickly dived again. There were 16 of them on the raft and a damaged raft lashed to it. They had no food and only a gallon flask of water which they agreed to ration to a fill of the cap each twice a day. The heat during the day was practically unbearable and they would climb overboard to cool off in the sea. Willie said they never thought that there might be sharks around. When they got too weak to climb in and out of the raft, they would scoop water over each other. The nights were cold.

Soon, men began to die. One man drank sea water and went mad, swimming away from the raft to his death. On the twelfth day the water ran out but as if by a miracle there was a thunderstorm on the following day, and they were able to refill the flask by catching the rainwater in a piece of canvas. Finally, on the sixteenth day they spotted a convoy of ships and raised a pole with a shirt on it to act as a flag and a tin can to catch the sun. A lookout on the ship escorting the convoy spotted the glint from the can and came alongside. By this time there were only nine men left and another died shortly after the rescue ship got them on board. The bosun also died a few days later.

Two other Whalsay men, Andrew Sandison and Dodie Irvine, were on the SS *Benarty* in 1940, carrying a cargo of tungsten from Rangoon to Britain when they were sunk in the Indian Ocean by the German raider *Atlantis*. They were kept on board the raider for 47 days, along with survivors from other ships she had sunk, over 300 of them and seriously overcrowded. They were eventually transferred to a captured Yugoslav tramp steamer, the *Durmitor*, which was carrying coarse salt. They were kept in the two rat-infested holds with the salt, 100 men in each. After 29 days at sea, they ran aground on a reef at the little coastal village of Warshikh in Italian Somaliland, just north of the capital, Mogadishu. They managed to get ashore and the following day were transferred to a prisoner of war camp in the capital. After two months there, they were transferred 50 miles down the coast to another camp in Merka, where they spent another month. The food consisted of macaroni and olive oil and sometimes bananas coated with syrup. Andrew's weight dropped from eleven stone to seven. Eventually, they were rescued by the British East African Corps, operating from Kenya to capture Italian Somaliland and Ethiopia from the Italians. When they finally set foot on Whalsay in April 1941, their wives had given up hope of ever seeing them alive again.

Lowrie Jamieson from Sandwick had a similar experience to Willie Anderson, in his case seventeen days in an overcrowded lifeboat in the Indian Ocean. There isn't much left now of the hospital in Mananjary, on the east coast of Madagascar, where Lowrie spent three weeks recovering from his ordeal, during which many of his shipmates died. His ship, the 10,000-ton *Fort Franklin*, had been on her way from Port Said on the Red Sea to Durban in South Africa, loaded with salt and sand as ballast, intending to take on a cargo of coal for Mauritius in Durban. At 0945 on 16th July, 1943, between the islands of Mauritius and Reunion, she was hit by two torpedoes from a German submarine and sank inside five minutes.

The chief engineer and four other engine room crew were killed by the impact of the torpedoes and another died from his injuries almost immediately after he was lifted aboard the lifeboat. One of the lifeboats was smashed in two. Lowrie initially got off onto a raft. The crew also managed to launch a small jolly boat, but it was slightly damaged, and the captain insisted that they all get into the one remaining lifeboat – 52 of them in the tiny wooden boat. Lowrie remembers the water lapping up almost to the gunwales and that periodically they all had to get out into the shark-infested water so she could be bailed out.

When they were in the lifeboat, the U-boat surfaced. She was the U-181 commanded by Wolfgang Luth, a U-boat ace who sank 10 ships in the Indian Ocean during this seven month voyage. He recorded the second highest tonnage of ships sunk of all the U-boat captains and was awarded Germany's highest military medal. The sinking of the *Fort Franklin* is mentioned in Jordan Vause's 1990 biography of Luth (*U-boat Ace. The Story of Wolfgang Luth*.) Lowrie was still on the raft when the U-boat surfaced but he was told that one of the officers asked for the usual information from the survivors – the name and tonnage of their ship, her cargo and origin and destination of the voyage. From Jordan Vause's book, this would probably have been the U-boat's doctor, Lothar Engel, who spoke good English.

The lifeboat had an engine, but it refused to start, and they had to rely on oars and a sail. After some alarming broaches before the following sea and near capsizes, Lowrie volunteered to take the helm as he was used with sailing open sailboats in rough seas as a fisherman in Whalsay. The mate had managed to salvage some charts and basic navigational equipment from the sinking ship, including a chronometer, but they managed to miss Reunion, their initial target. That left Madagascar, some 600 miles to the west as the next possible dry land. They had hard-tack biscuits and dried meat (pemmican) to eat and containers with fresh water but they soon discovered that some of them were contaminated and the contents undrinkable: water had to be rationed. By the last week this had been reduced to a teaspoonful each morning and evening. Some of the crew drank saltwater and went crazy, throwing themselves overboard. The captain sat holding a loaded pistol to guard the water supply.

They eventually made landfall north of Mananjary, with heavy surf breaking on the reef offshore. At Mananjary, there was a break in the reef and a narrow passage through the coastal sand dunes into a lagoon. Lowrie remembered a heart-stopping rush through the boiling surf to make the passage into the harbour. He thought the mate, a man called Evans, may have been in that port before as he seemed to know how to approach the entrance and Lowrie credited him with saving their lives. They were approached by a dhow. Lowrie remembered every-body scrambling on board the dhow except him, an Orkney boy around 20 years old (who had been on the *Fort Franklin* as an apprentice, intending to study for tickets) and one other crew member, as there wasn't room for them all. While they were waiting to be picked up, the Orkney boy had a look at the engine which wouldn't start, took out the spark plugs, cleaned them and the engine started immediately. The *Fort Franklin* had had steam engines. Lowrie observed drily that the surviving engine room crew were presumably not familiar with the mysteries of the internal combustion engine.

Lowrie wasn't sure how many of them survived, he thought about 30. He remembered being delirious and in agony as he was so dehydrated he couldn't urinate, his legs collapsing under him on the stone jetty where they landed. He was taken to the local hospital where he was looked after by a black doctor from Marti-nique in the West Indies. When he was discharged, he was billeted with a French coffee trader. The coffee was taken out through the harbour entrance to ships anchored offshore by dhows like the one which picked them up. Madagascar was a French colony then, previously under a Vichy government, which was in collaboration with the Nazis. However British forces had invaded from Kenya and supporters of General de Gaulle were now in control. Another Whalsay man, Henry Stewart, the former Shetland Islands Councillor, was on the island at the time with the British army but in those days, long before the mobile phone, Lowrie had no means of knowing this. The shipwrecked mariners had no money, but Lowrie remembered signing chits for drinks at the local club (whites only and no Vichy supporters). He had no idea who picked up the tab. After the war, Lowrie continued to sail and then emigrated to New Zealand in 1959. He died in 2017 aged 97.

Some others survived dangerous missions unscathed. Peter Anderson, Clate (Willie Anderson's brother) and Johnnie Kay, Sandwick, did a lone run (no convoy) to Murmansk on the SS *Empire Scott* in 1942. This was thought to be virtually a suicide mission getting supplies to the beleaguered Russians and the participants were later awarded medals.

In 1942 a military camp was built at Harlsdale, with radar equipment on the Wart of Clate. Between 80 and 100 servicemen were drafted in to operate the station. The radar housing, an engine house, gun emplacements and air raid shelters can still be seen on the Wart. The Harlsdale site has now been redeveloped for a council housing scheme and a shop, Tetley and Anderson, originally operating as a butcher shop managed by Wilfred Tetley, a Liverpudlian who had come up as the camp cook and married a local girl, Jasmine Anderson. The camp and the installations on the Wart were built using sand from the nearby Sands of Sandwick, a beautiful white beach of deep sand. Too much was taken and the beach is now just shingle. Along the coast to the west of the beach in Symbister Ness, a Catalina flying boat crashed into the cliffs. The crew of eight and two Russian envoys on board survived and were fed by Wilfrid Tetley before being taken away by an MTB.

During the war, commercial fishing activity virtually ceased. Men who would otherwise have been fishing manned the anti-submarine boom defences in Lerwick Harbour. Older men were in the Home Guard. But otherwise life went on. Rationing of food was in operation but its impact was less severe than most parts of the country because subsistence living was the order of the day anyhow from crofting produce and fish caught from the shore or close inshore by boys and old men. Everyone was issued with gas masks which fortunately were never needed but became interesting playthings for children after it was all over. The military camp was closed down. Wilfred Tetley stayed on as did Tammy Reid from Fife who also married a local girl, Babsie Anderson. Norman Burt, a radio operator from New Zealand, married local girl Ruby Anderson and they moved to New Zealand. Wilfie and Tammy quickly settled into island life, Wilfie setting up a butcher shop in one of the camp buildings and providing film shows every Saturday night in the Symbister Hall as well as acting as compere at local concerts. Tammy became the agent for goods being transported by the *Earl of Zetland*, the lifeline shipping service, looking after the water supply after piped water was provided around the island in 1953 and carted peats with his tractor and trailer from the peat hill to people's homes.

9

Infrastructure, Transport and Shipwrecks

Until the First World War, Whalsay didn't even have a road system, just a few tracks and a road of sorts serving the laird's farm and ending at the Spar Grind, just past Whitefield, near the Huxter Loch. In 1849 the laird offered to build a road from Kirkaness to Symbister in co-operation with the Destitution Board, set up to deal with poverty relating to the potato blight famine. Throughout Shetland and elsewhere in Britain and Ireland affected by the blight, men were employed building roads, rewarded with a day's supply of "meal" (flour) in return for a day's work – hence the name "meal roads." However, none of these were built in Whalsay and it is not known why the laird's offer was turned down.

During the First World War, a government sponsored scheme was brought in whereby the Zetland County Council took on unemployed fishermen to build roads. This resulted in the loop road from the Spar Grind to Isbister and then around to Symbister via Brough. Traewick was by-passed as one crofter refused to allow the road to pass through his land. Just after the war, the road was extended to Skaw. Gibbie Williamson from Marrister, who was born in 1903, recalled that this was his first job after leaving school. In 1930, Brough men worked together to lay a road from the Brough junction (Brough Grind) up to the Brough houses to enable the shop there to get its goods delivered by road instead of by boat from Symbister. This was extended past the Knowe and Creads in 1947 to complete the loop through to the junction with the main road at the Brough School. Peter Teeder Robertson laid a road to Nisthoose in 1923 to provide access to his shop there and it was taken over by the County Council in 1934. A road to Huxter was laid in 1934 and to Vevoe in 1937. In

Whalsay Harbour.

New Dock and adjacent buildings.

Fishermen at the Harbour, 1986.

Roll-on roll-off ferry the Linga.

Earl of
Zetland, *old
and new.*

the late 1950s and extending into the 1960s, a programme of road widening and tarring was carried out. The quarry at Sudheim employed around a dozen men in the summer, breaking rocks with 14lb hammers to feed the crusher. The foreman was Harry Anderson from Skerries.

A piped water supply finally arrived in 1953, using water from Buwater which was augmented by a dam. It had previously been used to supply the new Cruden housing scheme which was completed around 1950. Previously, people had relied on wells fed from springs, most crofts having their own one. There was a pump just behind the Bremen Booth at Symbister which people in that area used. Indoor toilets now began to appear using septic tanks but the old Elsan chemical toilets in outbuildings persisted into the 1960s. As the SIC's finances blossomed with the advent of money generated by the oil industry, the water supply system was progressively enhanced with the addition of a storage tank on a hill above Skaw, the building of a pumping station at the Huxter Loch to top up Buwater, the Livister Loch now also becoming part of the catchment area with a swift flowing burn feeding the Huxter Loch. Scottish Water took over responsibility for water and sewerage supply in Shetland from the SIC in the 1990s. In 2017 a complete overhaul of the system was completed, including a new pumping station at the Huxter Loch and refurbishment of the treatment works at Buwater.

The Cruden houses had a sewerage pipe discharging directly into the sea just north of the Pier House dock in Saltness. Sewerage systems with treated waste was provided for the various council housing schemes from the 1960s but more widespread schemes serving private houses mainly had to await the advent of oil money into the Shetland Islands Council's coffers in the 1980s and 1990s.

Elecricity didn't arrive until 1963 when a cable was laid from the Mainland to a landfall at Saltness. The military base at Harlsdale and the Wart had previously had their own generator but this was shut down at the end of the war. The advent of electricity enabled the introduction of refrigerators, which transformed food storage, as well as television and electrical appliances such as cookers and washing machines.

There was only one telephone in Whalsay at the time of the First World War, in the coastguard hut on the Wart operated by the Navy. The cable carrying the phone lines came ashore in Saltness. News about the war, including deaths, came by telegraph to the Post Office. Another cable was laid from Laxo on the Mainland to Saltness after the Second World War and a telephone was installed in the Post Office at the Maillands. In 1946, the District Council recommended that phones should be placed in the doctor's and nurse's houses and public phones at Skaw and Isbister to cater for medical emergencies. Kiosks were introduced in 1948 at Clate, Skaw, the Beach Lodge and Burnside (the Brough Post Office). Public phones were also provided in the porches of private houses at Toft (Robbie Anderson's ("Punch")), Marrister (Dodie Paton's) and Vevoe (Tammy Henry Simpson's). It wasn't until the 1960s that telephones became common in private houses, initially usually "party lines" which two houses shared. Manual exchange services were provided by the Irvine family at Barnpark and then Mary Grace Eunson from her house in the Crudens until an automatic exchange was built at Saltness to be replaced by the current digital one on the site of the former military camp at Harlsdale.

The original harbour, serving the German Hanseatic merchants, was at the east end of the beach at Symbister, with the Pier House and its adjacent dock, the Hame Dock. In the mid-19th century, a new dock was built by the laird at the west end of the beach, along with the Fish House and what is described as a carpenter's shed in the schedule attached to the listing of the dock, but later used to make barrels for herring. The two-storey building now known as the Net Store is described as the New Hoose in the listing schedule, as it was built later than the dock and other adjacent buildings, around 1900. It was originally used to store salt on the ground floor for Hay & Company's fishing operations with barrels stored on the upper floor. Its most recent use was for Andrew Jamieson's net mending business. The Fish House was used to store fish waiting to be shipped out of the island, kept fresh with ice gathered from ponds at the Mires of Marrister and near Nuckrawater and the Mill Loch at the Hillhead. A wooden pier extending out northwards from just below where the boating club now stands was destroyed in a gale in 1953, to be replaced by another extending westwards from the west end of the New Dock. Fishing boats were moored off in the voe, accessed by rowing boats. The North Voe was also used for anchorage.

In the 1950s pressure began to build up for a modern harbour to be built as the fishing fleet increased, added weight coming from the wrecking of the *Verdant* in a storm in January 1959 when she dragged her anchor and drove onto a small skerry on the Saltness side of the voe. A bitter debate arose between those who wanted the new harbour works to go in the South Voe and those who favoured the North Voe. Henry Stewart, who later became the Island's representative on the Shetland Islands Council, was an ardent advocate for the North Voe, but when that cause was lost became an equally ardent advocate for successive schemes in the South Voe. The first phase of the new harbour, a concrete pier stretching into deep water, sheltered by a substantial breakwater on the Symbister Ness side of the voe, was completed in 1964. In 1992, after years of advocacy at the SIC by Henry Stewart, the inner face of the breakwater was remodelled to create berthing space for purse netters and a sheltering breakwater built out from the Saltness side of the voe. As part of his campaign, in 1986, Henry assembled all the fishermen on the island for a photograph posed down at the harbour to illustrate how many families were dependent on it. As well as providing berthing space for fishing boats the harbour provides the ferry terminal and a sizeable marina for pleasure craft has been built with funding assistance from the SIC's Charitable Trust. The result is that it is now somewhat congested and a proposal arose to relocate the ferry operation to the North Voe. This reignited the old North Voe versus South Voe feud and the proposal was shelved. But it has not gone away and is still one of the options being considered along with a tunnel to the Mainland.

In the early 1970s an airstrip was built at Skaw funded mostly by money collected in the island. However, with the introduction of the car ferry system in 1975, it became largely redundant. The terminal building was used as a clubhouse by the golf club for a time and is now a private dwelling.

Transport to and from the island from 1877 to 1975 was provided by two *Earls of Zetland*, little coastal steamers. The first *Earl* was built for the newly formed Shetland Islands Steam Navigation Company on Clydeside. Even after being lengthened by 23 feet in 1884 she was still only 252 tons. She went into service in April 1877, initially serving a number of ports in Delting and Northmavine as well as the North Isles. In spite of her small size there was nowhere she could berth and goods were transferred on and off her by flitboats – sixareens or former ships' lifeboats. In 1890, the original company amalgamated with the Aberdeen based North Company to form the North of Scotland, Orkney and Shetland Steam Navigation Company. A new *Earl* arrived in August 1939, built in Aberdeen by Hall, Russell and Company. At 548 tons she was twice the tonnage of her predecessor and her relatively powerful diesel engines generated 850 horsepower, far outperforming the old *Earl*. However, with the onset of the Second World War, she was requisitioned by the navy as a troop carrier in the Pentland Firth, the old *Earl* continuing on the North Isles route until finally replaced once the war was over.

In 1975 the *Earl* was replaced by a roll-on, roll-off car ferry service operated by the council. Initially this was just one ferry operating to terminals at Laxo and Vidlin, the latter used in adverse weather conditions, especially when the wind was from a south-easterly direction. Later, a second ferry was provided enabling a service to be run every 45 minutes. Later still, with the arrival of the *Linga* to replace the original small ferry, the car-carrying capacity was substantially increased. Due to financial constraints on the council, the weekend service has now been reduced to one ferry, a source of discontent on the island and an incentive to have a tunnel option explored.

Records held by the Whalsay History Group record 41 shipwrecks around Whalsay, mainly on the small islands and skerries which fringe the main island, especially on the south and east sides. The earliest record is of a Norwegian ship which was wrecked on the Inner Holm of Skaw in AD 1500. The survivors, including two women, built a small chapel there as a thanksgiving for their delivery, the ruins of which can still be seen along with the grave of one of their shipmates who was not so lucky.

In 1780 a Russian frigate, the *Evststaffi*, was wrecked with the loss of all but six hands on Grif Skerry, off Isbister, where the haaf fishermen later had their out-station. In 1792, the *Nancy of London*, foundered off the east side of the island on her way from Norway to the Mediterranean with stockfish. The body of one of the crew, a Lerwick man called Francis Lyon, was washed up at the Ayre of

Breiwick and was buried there, where the grave can still be seen. On nearby East Linga, a Liverpool steamship the *Pacific* was wrecked in Snavi Geo in 1871, on a voyage from Norway to Hull, laden with timber. Two men were saved when the bowsprit lodged ashore and they were able to clamber along it to safety.

A brig from Danzig, now in Poland, was wrecked on the South Hoga Baa, to the south-east of Whalsay in 1817. Her crew reached the shore safely in two ship's boats. She was carrying a cargo of wheat, barley and peas bound for Liverpool. Six local men went off to try to salvage some of this but while they were on board the ship slipped off the rock and sank, drowning them all.

In 1884, a barque from Copenhagen, the *Alba*, carrying general cargo – beef, flour, sugar, rice, liquor, and prefabricated timber houses – to the Danish settlement at Inituk on the Davis Straits, north of Canada, was wrecked on the Flesheens of Sandwick. A crewman who survived said she was doing around 15 knots in heavy seas when she hit the rocks. There were 12 of a crew and seven passengers on board. All were lost except the mate, two crew men and one passenger who were taken off the rock by the sixareen, the *Mary*, from Sandwick, along with a pig and some tappet hens. The deckhouse which had been driven onto the rock and in which one of the survivors had sheltered during the night was later salvaged and sited down at the harbour in Symbister where it was known as the Toopic, where passengers waiting for the flitboat to take them out to the *Earl* used to shelter.

Apart from these disasters to passing ships, there have been a number of local tragedies. In 1795, a bridal party was lost coming back from Nesting. On Tuesday, 15th April, 1913, James Anderson, Tom Arthur and John Irvine left Symbister for Neep in Nesting to collect the mail. The mail was normally carried to the Northern Isles by the *Earl of Zetland* but when the steamer went south for her Board of Trade survey it was standard practice for the Whalsay mail to be collected from Nesting in open boats from Symbister. The crew were all experienced seamen, John Irvine the skipper of the fishing boat *Silver Spray*, James Anderson on the *George* and Tom Arthur on the *Topaz*. The boat was returning under sail when the southerly wind increased and the boat was seen to capsize and disappear. The men were never found but four days later the keel and bottom board of the hull and the buckled remains of the mast and sail were all washed ashore at the Groot of Stavaness in Nesting.

On the 12th August, 1842, a tragedy occurred for the people of the neighbouring island of Skerries when a boat carrying peats from Skaw to Skerries was lost with everyone on board, including women. There was no peat on Skerries so the people used to cast peats on Whalsay and ship them back to Skerries in boats. On this occasion two half-decked herring boats belonging to the laird, the *Corncrake* and the *Woodlark*, had gone across to load peats in the Sandy Geo near the Holm of Skaw. The *Corncrake* arrived back safely but the *Woodlark* foundered just off the South Mouth of Skerries Harbour with the loss of all eleven people on board.

10

Education, Religion and Health

The 1872 Education Act made schooling compulsory for seven to fourteen-year olds. The Livister school, built using stone from the Iron Age Fort across the Huxter Loch, had already opened, work having started on it in 1864. Before that, according to the author's grandmother, Mary Williamson (née Anderson), Andrew Hughson, who was blind, started a school in a barn at his house at Brough around 1840 and then moved it to an old house at Tripwell. He compensated for his lack of sight by having an astonishing memory. If someone read him a verse from the Bible, he could quote it back verbatim. His only textbook was the Bible. There was also a school in an old house at Toft in Isbister, now a sheep shelter, run by James Poleson (Peerie Uncle), who was almost a dwarf with bowlegs. The author's grandmother, who was born in 1865, attended Livister, walking nearly three miles across the hill from her home at the Burns, carrying a peat for the fire. The school hours were 10am to 4pm. The basic textbook was the Primer, which had the numbers up to ten and the alphabet. Later, they got Grieg's Arithmetic. Parents had to pay for schooling, including the teacher's wages. A new school was built at Livister in 1912, the original building being refurbished as a house for the teacher.

On the morning of the 19th April, 1906, the author's grandfather, Robert Anderson, who lived at Whitefield, in sight of the Livister School, realised that he hadn't seen the teacher, James Hill, moving around outside as usual. He went across to investigate and found no sign of him. As he was going off fishing, he told the School Board Clerk, George Irvine, what had happened and George organized a search party. In the afternoon, two Sandwick men took a rowboat off into the loch and came on the teacher's naked body floating face down in about six feet of water. He was known to have a drink problem but whether it was an accident or suicide was never

Livister School, Whalsay's first, built 1864.

Kirkaness with the Kirk and graveyard.

The Auld
Manse,
Marrister.

The Manse,
Marrister.

established. Another school was built at Brough in 1877 to serve the north end of the island. The first teacher was James Lutit. Teaching material was augmented by a book of Scottish history. The school was renovated and enlarged in 1936, a canteen built in 1945 and a secondary department two years later.

In 1964, education on the island was centralised when the Haa, Symbister House, was converted to a school. A new primary school was built nearby to the east in 1993.

John Stewart refers to four ancient chapel sites on Whalsay, one in Kirkaness, where the existing church is, another in Isbister where the Nisthouse houses are now, one at Symbister for which he doesn't specify a site and one on the Inner Holm of Skaw, believed to have been erected by the survivors of a shipwrecked Norwegian ship in 1500AD. The existing church was built in 1767 with an extension on the back added in 1887, when the original building was refurbished. The first resident minister was Angus Willans who arrived in 1870. He was accommodated in the Auld Manse which had previously been the home of the Lairds of Marrister. A new Manse was built in 1905 and sold as a private house when a new house was built for the minister in the 1990s.

The Church Hall at Saltness was built in 1905. Originally this was a joint venture between the community, who wanted a public hall, and the church but following a dispute it has been used purely for church business since the 1920s. David Harbison, who was the minister on the island during the 1960s, was responsible for a resurgence in football and was instrumental in getting a cinder pitch laid at Bellsbrae (Tammy's Park) which opened in 1962. He was a speedy left winger who represented Shetland in the annual "international" against Orkney (although his shots on goal tended to fly heavenwards like his prayers) as well as being probably the most popular minister the island ever had. In 2019, the Church of Scotland announced a rationalisation of their buildings to be used for worship, in the face of declining congregations and the high cost of maintaining a very large building stock. In Whalsay, the kirk at Kirkaness is no longer to be used, all religious activity to be conducted in the Church Hall at Saltness.

The Whalsay History Group hold records of visiting doctors from Nesting/Lunnasting from as early as 1855 when a Doctor John Seeland is mentioned. In 1903, a Dr Burgess moved to Whalsay, staying at the Old Manse until he left in 1914. He was followed over the next 5 years by Doctors Chattergee and Ojo Olaribigbe (a Nigerian) who both lived and had their surgeries in Bellsbrae House (Buckfit's). Dr Wilson followed from 1920 to 1925. He was accompanied by the island's first nurse, Nurse Barry. Dr Wilson fell in a stiggie (alley way) at Brough and lay there all night, after which he was no longer able to work. The nurse left with him. The next two long-staying doctors, Dr Pyle (1925-29) and Dr Orr (1931-38) stayed with Betty Krosky at Anchor Cottage and had their surgeries there until a doctor's house was built near the Symbister Hall in 1932. Dr Helen Potter was in post from 1943 until the National Health Service came into operation in 1948. In 1963 Dr Alex Mack arrived. His wife, Mary, was also a doctor. In April 1964, his body was found in his car in an old quarry at Nukrawater, with a hose pipe leading from the exhaust into the vehicle. His wife remained on the island to carry on the practice. In 1974, Brian Marshall arrived as a relatively newly qualified doctor and stayed in the post until he retired, remaining on the island to pursue his life-long hobby of ornithology. The old doctor's house was demolished in the 1980s and replaced by a new house and surgery at the North Park which now also houses a dentist.

In the days before there was a nurse on the island, babies were delivered by "howdie" women, the most famous of whom were Girsie (Gracie) Williamson and her daughter Janie Irvine, known as "Midder Janie." In 1936, a public meeting was held to set up a Nursing Association with the aim of raising funds to bring a nurse to the island on a permanent basis. Nurse Mckenzie came in April 1937 followed by Nurse MacDonald from 1938-40. During the Second World War, May Steedman (née Irvine), the first Whalsay girl to qualify as a nurse (in England) did some relief work (She also worked in Foula at this time). A nurses' house was built in 1939 just across the road from the Brough School.

11

Shops, Industry and Leisure Facilities

Records held by the Whalsay History Group show that there have been a surprising number of shops in the island since the laird surrendered his monopoly to Hay & Company in 1864 when they took over the shop at Symbister. The most northerly shop was run by James Poleson at Zoar in the early 1990s but didn't last long. The Brough area has had four shops, those kept by Tammy Hutchison at Newtoon from 1898 to 1903 and the branch of Pete's of Lerwick managed by Gibbie Arthur from 1932 to 1939, were equally short-lived but the Brough Shop started in the 1890s by Willie Anderson endured until 1983 and became something of an institution under Willie's daughter Jessie and her husband Willie Polson. The Sunday night "talking shop" was attended by the men of the township including notable comedians like Henry Williamson, whose humorous poetry about local events was enjoyed throughout the island, Lowrie Simpson, (Mootie's Lowrie), originally from Skaw and Peter o' Lee, who could be relied on for an acrimonious argument about almost anything. Hay & Company had a branch at Tripwell from the early 1900s until they sold out at Symbister in 1951 and closed their branch as well.

Marrister had a shop from the early 1900s until 1937 operated by William Sandison. Isbister has had four shops over the years, the first, run by George Leask at Toft from the late 1890s to the early 1900s, was short-lived. In 1930 Walter Robertson opened Hillside Stores in Grunnataing which he ran until 1944 when he moved to Lerwick and ended up running Solotti's iconic ice cream shop there. After he left, his shop was taken over by the Co-op (SCWS) until it closed down in 1951. Babs Hughson (née Polson), who had managed the Co-op, then set up a shop in her own house but it closed in 1955. Peter Theodore Robertson (Peter Teeder) also had

The Arthur's Shop, Sudheim, now the Auld Shop.

J. & M. Shearer's herring station at Symbister.

Leisure Centre, built 1990.

Golf Club, Skaw – Britain's most northerly.

Pleasure boat marina.

Regatta boats.

Fernlea Care Centre, Marrister.

a shop in Isbister from the 1920s until 1945 when he too moved to Lerwick. There is a story about one of his confrontations with a client who wanted to buy salt. She said "I'm needin' saat, Peter." He replied "We hae nae saat petre." She persisted, "But it's saat, Peter." By this time Peter was losing his rag and came back "I'm tellin' dee, wuman, we hae nae saat petre." (Salt petre was used in curing sheep skins.)

The Arthur family started a shop in their house at Sudheim in the early 1900s, later moving it to an adjacent building known as the Auld Shop. In 1935 they built a new shop up at the road. It closed down after "Young" Jamie Arthur's death in 2004 but has recently been resurrected by Misty Di Angeli, who bought the Arthur's property, as a gift shop and café.

Gifford and Dodie Irvine had a shop at the Hillhead from 1920 to 1937 and Robert and Mimie Nicolson one at the Maillands from the 1920s to the late 1940s. Robbie Stewart started a business breeding hens and selling eggs from a premises at Sandwick in the early 1940s, later diversifying into groceries. After his death in 1976, the business was taken over by Mimie Williamson (nee Irvine) until it closed down in 1991.

The Co-op opened a shop in one of the redundant RAF Camp buildings at Harlsdale in 1949 with Wilfred Tetley as manager. This building was closed down in 1970 as the site was to be redeveloped for SIC housing and the Co-op moved its business to Bellsbrae House (Buckfit's). When the Co-op closed down their operations in Whalsay, Henry Stewart, who had been their manager, took it over until it closed in 1989. In another redundant building at the Harlsdale Camp, Wilfred Tetley set up a butcher shop in 1955 with his partner Geordie Anderson – Tetley & Anderson. They slaughtered animals, including cows, in the butcher's house at Dimmie Geo down at the banks (cliffs) below Clate. After Geordie left the partnership to go back to the fishing, Wilfie diversified into general groceries. After his death in 1987 the shop was taken over by Iris Anderson (nee Shearer) then Anne Marie Anderson and it remains as one of the two surviving groceries on the island.

There had been other butcher shops on Whalsay before Tetley and Anderson. Johnie Shearer had one at Clate from 1938 until the late 1940s, using the butcher house at Dimmie Geo. Prior to that, Jamie Sinclair had a butcher shop at Skibberhoull from 1911 to 1932. The only other specialist shop which has operated on the island is Leasks Electrics, the business originally developed by Magnie Leask at Harsdale and the shop built by his nephew George Magnus Leask in 1982, but this ceased trading in 2012. In the early 1990s, SHOARD, a group seeking to support disabled children on the island, set up a charity shop in the former Brough School which attracts customers from all over Shetland.

All these small grocer shops supplied a fairly basic menu of goods as until the 1960s most people were still relying for most of their food stuff on the produce of the sea and the croft. The staple goods were flour, oatmeal, sugar, salt, paraffin for lamps and tar for roofs. Gradually this diversified with relative luxuries like bread, butter, cheese, jam, biscuits, tinned food and sweeties. Until after the First World War, when the loop road around the island was built, the shops at Isbister and Brough had to be supplied by sea. The first motor vehicle, Hay & Company's Ford lorry, didn't appear until 1925.

For many years, Hay & Company dominated the commercial life of the island. The business they took over from the laird in 1864 included the shop, fishing and kelp operations, all for a rent of £100 per annum. An extension was built onto the shop to house the Post Office. Until the haaf fishing petered out in the 1880s, Hay & Company continued to cure fish – ling, cod and tusk - on the beaches at Symbister and the North Voe and East Linga as long as Grif Skerry was being used as an out-station. Whitefish was bought to and preserved in the Fish House with ice from ponds on the island. As well as barrelling salted herring, a kippering kiln was operated from 1887. Oil was extracted from fish livers and whale oil produced. Whales were "caaed" ashore elsewhere in Shetland and shipped to Whalsay for processing by boiling. The oil was used in lamps. The oil extraction business was closed down in 1912 when the Company decided to concentrate on herring curing and moved the oil operation elsewhere. Hay & Company processed nearly all Shetland's kelp by the 1870s. Tangles were collected after winter storms and drift weed in May. It was dried and burned in pits. Fifty to sixty tons were exported annually for use in the glass and soap industries. The kelp business was closed down after the First World War due to shipping difficulties and new products replacing it. After they bought a half ton Ford lorry in 1925, they were able to transport goods around the island. With the placement of some benches in the back, it doubled up as a taxi.

Hay & Company's first manager at Symbister was John Nicolson, who was succeeded by David Williamson, who lived in the renovated Beach Lodge. When John Nicolson retired, he moved the Post Office to his house at the Maillands at the other end of the beach from the shop. The last two joint managers were known as Hackie and Batty, sounding like a stand-up comedy pairing but actually Hercules Williamson and Barclay Jamieson. The company sold out to J&M Shearer in 1951 who had rented the herring station from them since 1922. Shearers then sold the shop on to John William Johnson from Skerries and it is still operated by his son Bobby and grandson Alastair as JWJ Ltd. There is an amusing story about John William taking on Jamie Leask, (a brother to the famous Lerwick character, Whalsay Willie) to help around the shop and store. Jamie was considered to be a bit simple minded and this was really just a charitable act on John William's part. John William explained what the job would involve to Jamie and told him that he would get a week's holidays every year. Jamie replied "Dat soonds fine. I'll mebbe tak me holy week first." Perhaps he wasn't all that simple minded after all.

Ian Anderson built a pub, "Oot Ower", with associated holiday chalets, in 2001, next door to the former Livister School. This remains the only public licensed premises on the island, the other licences being for the boating and golf clubs. When it opened, the Oot Ower operated a restaurant but that has now been reduced to a Sunday night service by a Lerwick based Chinese restaurant. There is a café with limited opening hours in the gift shop which was formerly the Arthurs' Shop and the youth club provide a café in their premises in the former Livister School at weekends. The Symbister Hall has occasional Sunday teas for fund-raising purposes during the summer. But there are no full-time restaurants or cafes on the island, an obstacle to promoting further growth in tourism.

In 1947 the main post office moved from the Maillands to the Beach Lodge, where it was run by Maggie Leask and then moved to the Leask family's house at Harlsdale where it was operated by Maggie, her brother Bertie and his wife Maggie Jean until they retired and it was taken over by Tetley and Anderson's shop in 1991. The Brough Post Office, serving the north end of the island, was run from 1936 to 1961 by Mary Hughson as postmistress and her husband Tammy as postman from their house, Burnside, opposite the Brough School. When they retired, their daughter-in-law Babs

Hughson (neé Poleson) took over. It moved to the Houll Grind in 1968 where Cathy Simpson (neé Bruce) was postmistress and then back to Burnside in 1986 where Babs again became postmistress. It was centralised at Tetley and Anderson's in 1994 when Babs retired.

A policeman was posted to Whalsay in 1980 with a house in the Crudens allocated to him, a portacabin being used as the station. A purpose-built police station was built adjacent to the leisure centre around 2014. However, shortly afterwards the island's resident policeman was withdrawn and law enforcement is carried out by officers visiting from mainland Shetland. A fire service was introduced in the early 1960s staffed by local volunteers, their very basic equipment housed in a small hut next to the Skeo on the beach at Symbister. The hut was replaced in the early 1980s by a purpose-built fire station at the Hillhead and in 2013 by a new, larger one, next door to the Church Hall at Saltness, handy for dealing with any hell fire preaching next door.

Knitting had long been a part-time activity for women on the island, their "sock" (knitting) never out of their hands in moments of inactivity and even when doing other things like "dyaan ta stack" (going to fetch peats from the hill.) The Hanseatic merchants had bought knitted goods such as socks as did the Dutch herring fishermen. Fair Isle knitting is believed to have started in the 1920s. The first knitting machine arrived around 1940 and the Fair Isle machine around 1970. John Tait set up a knitwear factory in the disused Brough School in 1970 but it closed in 1986. At the turn of the 20th century, an experiment was tried with growing flax at the Lintihouse (another name for flax) to make linen cloth but it was unsuccessful.

As well as the knitwear factory, John Tait opened a fish processing business at the Brough School in 1970 and then built a new factory at Symbister Ness which operated until 2011. Initially, the factory processed whitefish but after John Tait had to retire for health reasons, it changed over to processing salmon. Its closure, largely due to difficulties with ferry costs and capacity, was a major blow for employment on the island, especially for women. Ian Irvine from Skibberhoull took over the vacant building as a workshop for his engineering business. He also took over the former salmon hatchery buildings above Newtoon, on a burn flowing from the Houll Loch, which Peter Lowrie Williamson had established in the 1980s but had to close due to persistent problems with disease. John Ward Irvine built a workshop for panel-beating and paint spraying near the Houll Loch in 1993. Angus Irvine had a motor vehicle repair business at Boothpark from the 1960s until his premature death in 2000. His brother, Magnie, in partnership with Hecky Simpson, Nisthouse, had a building firm, Simpson and Irvine from 1972 until 1993 and built many houses on the island. There are a number of small firms involved in building and maintenance and earth-moving work, but major jobs tend to be dominated by firms from outside Whalsay.

Over the years, Whalsay has built up an impressive range of leisure facilities. The first public hall was built at Isbister in 1909 followed by the Symbister Hall in 1932. Both have taken advantage of money available from the SIC's Charitable Trust from 1978 for extensions and refurbishment. The Shetland Recreational Trust, funded by the Charitable Trust, provided a leisure centre in 1990, with a 15-metre swimming pool and large games hall, at a cost of around £2 million. The year it opened, over 60,000 people used its facilities with a further 8,000 children through the education department's use of the centre. This is thought to be a British record per head of population for a facility of this type. The centre employs 14 people full time and a few others part-time.

Sports available on the island include sailing (model yachts as well as regatta boats), football, golf, tennis, angling, netball, bowls, badminton, trampolining and swimming. Women's hockey is popular, and the island has one of the top teams in Shetland but there is no pitch on the island. Recreational fishing is available from the marina in Symbister Harbour. Several of the island's lochs provide good trout fishing and a number of aficionados take part in competitions on mainland Shetland. Badminton, netball and bowls are played in the leisure centre which is also used for trampolining and the island has produced a junior Scottish champion at this sport, Karis Irvine. Badminton had been popular since after the Second World War, played in the Symbister Hall. Tennis courts were provided with the conversion of the Haa to a school but are little used, climatic conditions not helping.

At one time, particularly in the 1960s and 1970s, the annual regatta was the highpoint of the social year with nearly thirty boats participating in Linga Sound. Lunches of boiled mutton were provided for the sailors on board the flagship, the Research, anchored off in the South Voe. Men from all over the island would congregate at Symbister dressed in collar and tie. The regatta dance was the biggest one of the year. It all began in 1903 when the Whalsay Boating Club was formed. At the first regatta, nine boats competed in the lugsail races, six in the "muckle" squaresail and five in the "peerie" squaresail. There were three rowing races. The following year there was a swimming race, not to be repeated for another 50 years. By 1925 there were 40 boats. In 1931 there was a football match between the newly formed Whalsay Thistle Club and a Lerwick team. In 1939, the original boating club was dissolved, after a dispute among the participants in the sport, and a new organization, Whalsay Boating and Sports Club, created. (Land sports had been introduced in 1913.)

In the early years, the *Cormorant*, owned by Jamsie Irvine of Symbister, was the boat to beat. The Inter-club Regatta in Lerwick was started in 1948 and Whalsay participated from the start. The *White Wings*, built by Davie Bruce of Skaw in 1955 for Robbie Williamson was the last ballasted boat built and the last to continue competing. In 1958 the *Silver Spray* was built for Glybbie's Lowrie (Irvine) and dominated the sport for the next three decades. Lowrie's son, Peerie Lowrie, had the *Sceptre* built in the early 1960s and soon began giving his father a run for his money. The two of them paired for the inter-club team race in 1971, won it for Whalsay for the first time in 21 years. By the 1980s there were nearly 30 boats. There was a move away from ballasted to unballasted boats, hulls became longer and faster and more lightweight. Greatly improved sails were bought, seriously increasing the costs of the sport.

In the 1990s there was a steep decline in the number of boats, the old-style boats being outclassed by the new, sleeker models. By the end of the 1990s, there were less than 10 boats left, competing for nearly 30 cups and trophies. The 21st century has been dominated by Peerie Lowrie's son, Lawrence, and his son Christopher is already showing promise of carrying on this family's remarkable domination of the sport into the fourth generation. Sadly, the days of mass public participation in sailing as participant and spectator are gone but for the crews involved in the sport it has reached a much more professional level in the standard of boats and gear used. (A sail now costs over £1,000.) There are twice-weekly races and a team sent to the annual Inter-Club Regatta in Lerwick, again a much reduced event in recent years. In 1983 the Boating Club built a licensed clubhouse on the former herring station at Symbister. They also have a concrete launching ramp adjacent to the New Dock. Model yachts are sailed in the Houll Loch in winter. An access road has been provided with European Union grant aid and an equipment hut provided. The path around the loch has been upgraded with aid from the SIC and now provides a popular walk for the general public as well as serving the model yacht club.

Football has a long history on the island going back to the time of Peter a Banks (Peter Robertson) in the 1930s but hampered by the absence of a suitable pitch until 1962. Peter had emigrated to Australia and set up a boat building business. Timber began disappearing from the yard, so Peter decided to carry out surveillance one night. During the night a van appeared and he saw his night watchman selling timber to the driver. In the ensuing confrontation, Peter brained his watchman with a shovel and killed him. A friend of his, who was the skipper of a ship in the port, hid Peter and then smuggled him back to Britain, where he returned to the Banks, just below Brough, abandoning his wife in Australia. Shortly after his return, he started to organise football on the island and at a meeting on 26th November, 1930, Whalsay Thistle Football Club was formed, playing their first game against Lerwick Thistle in April, 1931.

These early games were played on the Lubba, a piece of rough, stoney ground at the Houll Grind, just east of the Brough houses. Peter is best known for a speech he made at Sandwick (the one on the Mainland) following a match which the Whalsay team played there. Pontificating on tactics he said: "Every man haes ten yairds and ten tens is a hunder an' ten – every blody hell's feul tyeens dat. If duy dunnoo wirk as a team an' pluy as a team, duy moight as weel poo up da goalposts an' shite aa hols." The players during this era must have reached a reasonable standard of skill. When Willie a Tip (Hutchison) was called up to work in the coal mines in Fife as a "Bevan Boy", he got a trial with the local professional club, Dunfermline. Organised football on the island effectively came to an end in 1946. After that, an even more unsuitable pitch at the North Park was occasionally used for local games such as the traditional married men versus single but it took the arrival in 1958 of a new minister, David Harbison, a keen player himself, to galvanise the community into action and work towards providing a cinder pitch at Bellsbrae Park (Tammy's Park). It was opened on 20th October, 1962, at a cost of £3,000. Ten years later the cinders were covered with earth to make a grass pitch which was further refurbished in 1983. In August 2002 a new synthetic surface, all-weather pitch was opened at a cost of nearly a million pounds, (funded from local fund raising, the SIC and its Charitable Trust, and the Sports Scotland Lottery Fund), adjacent to the new Primary School. Appropriately, it was named after and opened by David Harbison, who had been instrumental in getting the old pitch at Bellsbrae.

Whalsay now participates in all the Shetland-wide competitions. Peter a' Banks can at last rest easy in his grave at Kirkaness. But the 2019 season did not go well for the local team, ending near the bottom of the main league and not winning the Parish Cup. You could imagine Peter turning in his grave and muttering "Doy moight as weel dyeen inta likweedoyshin lik Bury; efter aa dir bun ployin pish aa season." Karl Williamson , (Mary Williamson's great-grandson) signed for Aberdeen as a 16-year-old and later played for Brechin City. Michael Williamson from Whitefield was Whalsay's most prolific goal scorer ever and represented Shetland as a striker against the old enemy Orkney in the annual inter-county matches for a number of years.

Whalsay has the most northerly golf course in Britain. The course was laid out in the early 1970s following the purchase of a disused croft at Skaw Taing. A licensed clubhouse was completed in 1996. The size of their membership now probably makes golf the most popular sport on the island. Over the years, Whalsay has produced a lot of talented musicians. Traditionally, fiddle playing was the outlet for this talent. In the early 1900s, Tammy Hughson, from Toft in Isbister, was renowned for his fiddling. Later, he was succeeded by Auld Glybbie (Johnnie Irvine) and then from the 1950s by Gibbie a Creads (Hutchison) and Alan Tulloch (Brough.) In the 1960s and 70s a local band was formed playing Scottish country music at dances and weddings. This array of fiddle, accordion and guitar players included the three Arthur brothers, Tammy, Davie and Willie, Peerie Lowrie Irvine, (a self-taught maestro on the accordion), Alan Tulloch and Magnie Leask (Harlsdale). Around 1965, Whalsay's first pop group, The Lockerboard Union, was started by the "fab four" Ian Hutchison (Hamister), the lead vocalist, Brian Poleson (Huxter) on drums, Willie a Knowe (Hutchison), and Hughie Anderson (Stuartbrae) on guitars. Around this time, a disused croft house at Sandwick, known as Muckle Beenie's after the last inhabitant, operated as a "shebeen" for the local youth at weekends, which, with the pop group, gave Whalsay a touch of the famous 1960s youth culture. Anyone who can remember it wasn't there. The 21st century has seen something of a renaissance in music on the island with a number of talented fiddlers emerging both male and female. Two groups, the Bashies and Small Hours have taken over from the Lockerboard Union and perform all over Shetland, even producing CDs.

12

Population, People,
Places and Folklore

Whalsay managed to hold its population from Shetland's peak of over 31,000 in 1861, while the rest of Shetland suffered severe depopulation, dropping to an all-time low of 17,812 in 1961. During this period Whalsay actually gained population, rising from 728 in 1861 to 872 in 1961. By 2011 there were 1061 people on the island, and it has remained over 1,000 in spite of a reduction in the size of the whitefish fleet and closure of the fish factory. There are two main reasons for this buoyancy. Firstly, Whalsay retained its fishing industry while other parts of Shetland gave up in despair after successive disasters at the Haaf fishing in the 19th century. Secondly, the lairds did not resort to "clearances" of crofters to make way for extensive sheep grazing as happened elsewhere in Shetland. Indeed they took measures to retain men on the island to fish for them, such as the "truck system" which kept men constantly in debt to them and hence obliged to continue fishing for them with draconian penalties for men who defied this system such as exile from the island for going to the Greenland whale fishery, as happened to two Vatshoull men. While some of the lairds were tyrants, and from time to time exiled crofters from the island for alleged misdemeanours such as failing to pay their rent, some of their schemes were quite enlightened for the time.

The setting up of the farm in 1863 actually created jobs as people were brought into the island to work on it. Far from being dedicated to extensive sheep grazing, the farm had 100 acres under cultivation in 1871. The building of new croft houses at Brough, Clate, Sandwick and Challister around 1840 improved crofters' living conditions and probably reduced the temptation to emigrate. In more recent times, Whalsay fishermen mostly resisted the temptation of well-paying jobs at Sullom Voe building the oil terminal, which decimated the Burra Isle fishing fleet.

Brough houses built by the laird in the 1840s.

Brough houses built by the laird in the 1840s.

Isbister, thought to be the earliest Viking settlement on the island.

Cruden Houses, the first council housing scheme, built 1949.

Anchor Cottage, built in late 19th century by an Arthur family and later lived in by Betty Croskie who kept doctors and other visiting gentry.

Bellsbrae House, Hillhead (Buckfit's) built by Jamie Shearer in 1906 and used to house doctors.

Da Glybe, where Midder Janie, the "howdie wife" lived for a time and later Nora, an Irishwoman.

Grieve's House, Sudheim, where Hugh MacDiarmid lived in the 1930s, now a Shetland Amenity Trust camping bod.

Traewick after the people had left.

Until the 1950s, the settlement pattern remained much the same as had been established in Viking times. Clate and Sandwick were not part of the farm and had their own scattald, shared with Huxter. The Sandwick Loch area appears to have been an important settlement area in Neolithic and Bronze Age times. The plantie crubs around the loch are a sure sign that Neolithic house sites once proliferated, and the burnt mounds indicate that settlement there continued into the Bronze Age. There are foundations of what appears to be a stone circle just south of the largest burnt mound. The Flesheens of Sandwick was where the Danish ship the *Alba* met her fate in 1884. During the Second World War the Wart of Clate was used to site a radar station.

The Harlsdale area was part of the farm and during the Second World War, the location of the military camp serving the radar station on the Wart. After the war, one of the camp buildings housed the Co-op shop and later another a butcher shop, later converted to a general store. The Post Office also operated from Harlsdale in the post-war period before re-locating in the shop there. The digital telephone exchange building was also located within what had been the RAF camp.

The Hillhead is dominated by the Haa and its associated buildings. The buildings surrounding the courtyards around the Haa housed livestock in the Midden Court and horses and workshops around the outer courtyard, where the flour mill was also found, now converted to a private house. The mill was driven by water from the Mill Loch, now filled in, following the accidental drowning of a little girl, Alison Stewart. Part of the buildings around the outer courtyard has been renovated by the Whalsay History Group to form a Heritage Centre. They have long-term plans to rehabilitate the whole strip of buildings. Across the road to the east stands Bellsbrae House or Buckfit's built in 1906 by James Shearer, a founder member of J&M Shearer, the herring barreling company. This substantial two-storey building was used to lodge professional people on the island such as doctors. It was later occupied by Captain Tammy Shearer who taught navigation at the Brough school. The strip of four attached cottages known as the Bothies below the mill were built to house incoming farm workers. Just to the east of the Haa complex, the leisure centre was built and later a new primary and infant school. A new artificial surface football field was also developed here, replacing Bellsbrae (Tammy's) Park up above.

Symbister, Southern Farm in Old Norse, is believed to be one of the earliest Viking settlements. It was where the lairds got their first foothold on the island. Their first mansion, the Auld Haa, built in 1702, stands at the head of the Böd Walk. Behind it to the south, a strip of four attached houses were built to accommodate incoming farm workers. Down by the sea, German merchants had two trading booths, Hamburgers in the restored Pier House and the Bremen Booth, now a private house. An artificial beach, created to dry fish and cutting off Leebie's Loch to the south, extends to the "New" Dock, built around the mid 19th century, with the new harbour beyond. In the 1950s, a bitter feud developed between people who wanted to develop a new harbour in the North Voe and those who wanted to continue developing the South Voe at Symbister. Henry Stewart, who later became Whalsay's representative on the Shetland Islands Council, was an ardent North Voe supporter. He lost that battle but then put his heart and soul into arguing the case for substantial amounts of money to be spent building a new harbour at Symbister. The first phase, a new concrete pier and sheltering breakwater, was completed in 1964. Henry again led a campaign for work to face up the inner side of the breakwater to create berthing space for purse netters and build another breakwater from the Saltness side of the Voe, providing additional shelter. As part of this campaign, he commissioned a photograph of the assembled masses of Whalsay fishermen down by the harbour, to illustrate the number of people depending on it.

A recent proposal to move the ferry terminal to the North Voe has to some extent rekindled the old feud from the 1950s. Whalsay's first shop, initially operated by the Laird until taken over by Hay & Company, stands just across the Böd Walk from the Bremen Booth. It also housed the Post office until it moved to the Maillands at the other end of the beach. The public hall was built in 1932 at the top of the Böd Walk and just to the east, a house for the doctor. In 1983, the boating clubhouse was built on part of the site of the former herring curing station. During the Napoleonic Wars, navy press gangs used to raid the islands kidnapping men for the warships. During that war, it was estimated that there were over 3000 Shetlanders serving in the navy, many of whom never came home. Down near the harbour in Symbister Ness, there had been a steep sided narrow cleft in the cliff face called Kirny Dyeo, dyeo (geo) being the dialect name for this sort of feature and "kirny" meaning "churny" from the churning of the sea when it surged into the narrow mouth of the dyeo. There was a local legend that a man had jumped across the dyeo to escape the press gang. It would have been an Olympic standard jump but then life in the Royal Navy in those days was no picnic. Kirny Dyeo is no longer there. It disappeared during the quarrying operations to build the adjacent harbour.

Saltness, where presumably, sometime in the past, salt had been made, was part of the laird's farm until it was broken up in 1903 and the present pattern of crofts created. There had been a broch there in Iron Age times and a German bod. The church hall was built there in 1905, the new fire station building now standing beside it. It is not known who the skipper was that gave his name to Skibberhoull. The North Beach was another artificial creation to dry fish. The sea would previously have extended inland as far as Skibberhoull Knowe.

A wide valley extends the width of the island from Skibberhoull to the Huxter Loch. Sudheim (erroneously spelled Sodom on Ordnance Survey maps) was home to Hugh MacDiarmid when he lived in Whalsay in the 1930s. A poet and journalist, (his real name was Christopher Grieve and he was known as "Auld Grieves" in Whalsay) he arrived in the summer of 1933 with his second wife Valda Trevlyn and young son Michael. At first, they lived in Anchor Cottage with Betty Krosky where Doctor Orr was also living. He and the doctor became drinking buddies. The house they moved to at Sudheim was very poorly furnished, the bed made of tea chests and they stored their belongings in orange boxes obtained from the nearby shop. They were very poorly off – Valda used to gather "grice mites" (tiny potatoes left when the tatties were taken up) from the rigs and birds' eggs from the banks (cliffs). On one occasion, when MacDiarmid went off fishing with one of the local boats, he was so hungry he took a bite out of the back of a raw herring. Neighbouring families used to take pity on young Michael and give him something to eat. MacDiarmid didn't mix much with the local people, socializing with the local "gentry" – the doctor, minister, teachers and the laird and his visitors. The laird was his bridge partner. He was fond of a "dram" and one Burns' Supper in the Symbister Hall was particularly notorious – "Smithy", the Livister School head-master, staggered into the dyke across from the hall when they left, broke his fiddle and lost his glasses. MacDiarmid had to be helped home by two men.

In 1928 he had helped found the Scottish National Party (his entry in *Who's Who* included Anglophobia among his hobbies). While in Whalsay in 1934 he joined the Communist Party but was expelled in 1937, rejoined and was expelled again. From 1931 to 1943 he was watched by the British Intelligence Services as a suspected communist sympathiser. He wrote some of his best poetry while in Whalsay, including "On a Raised Beach", inspired by a visit to West Linga. His "synthetic Scots" language is difficult to digest but he is among Scotland's best-known poets. In 1935 he suffered a nervous breakdown and Doctor Orr sent him south to a psychiatric hospital near Perth. He recovered and returned to Whalsay that same year. He was later joined by Grant Taylor who had volunteered to act as his secretary on a bed and board basis to catch up with the backlog of books he had been commissioned to write and his financial situation improved. The government were obviously keeping an eye on him and in 1942 he received a letter from them under their wartime "industrial conscription" policy to work in a munitions factory in Glasgow.

Sudheim was also where the Arthur family started a shop. Whitefield, to the east, may have got its name from the bog cotton which used to proliferate on the flat, peaty ground down towards the Muckle Burn. Two attached shepherds' cottages were built here for the farm, the easternmost one replicating the old Viking style with the barn and byre attached to the gable. Opposite Whitefield, in the hills just across the valley, there was a deep hollow in the peat called the Holl ida Sneugins – the Sneugins being the name of the hills. Local legend held that men used to hide from the Press Gang there. In those days it would have been covered with heather, long since gone through burning to improve grazing for sheep and in the process of cutting peat to dry for fuel.

Livister is another old Viking settlement, the name meaning "Leavings" or land left over. Whalsay's first school was built here in 1864, using stone from the Iron Age fort across on the other side of the Huxter Loch. When the school moved to Symbister House the school buildings were converted to a Youth Centre and the schoolhouse (the original school building) to a private house. Early in the 21st century, the Oot Ower pub was built beside the old school buildings. Huxter, sits on the hill above Livister. Its name derives from the Old Norse word for "mound" and there are a number of Neolithic age remains to corroborate this some of which have been obliterated by crofting activity.

Hamister means harbour farm in Old Norse, referring to its location above the North Voe. Just to the east of the most easterly croft there is what appears to be the site of a Viking water mill on Stiki's Burn, "stiki" meaning "dam" in Old Norse. Anchor Cottage, a substantial, two-storey building, was built in the late 19th century by an Arthur family. It is not known where they got the money for such a large house. It was later bought by Betty Krosky (nee Elizabeth Williamson from Brough) who had married a Captain Hutchison who worked as a pilot in China and made a lot of money. When he died, his wife married a Pole called Krosky who managed to embezzle her money. She presumably had enough left to buy Anchor Cottage and run it as a boarding house, known as Krosky's, keeping a succession of doctors including Doctor Orr, a good friend of Hugh MacDiarmid.

Marrister, meaning horse farm in Old Norse, had its own peerie laird until it was merged with the Symbister estate in 1836 through intermarriage between the two families. It seems likely that there was a German trading post there, a house down by the sea being called the Böd. Marrister housed the local ministers with both the Old and New Manses being located there as well as the current minister's house. The ten-bed Fernlea or Wishart and Anderson Care Centre, built by the Shetland Islands Council's Charitable Trust in 1992, is also located there. There are no stories recorded about the Gallow Hill rising above Marrister but witches were persecuted elsewhere in Shetland in the 17th century so it is quite possible that the hill was used for that purpose. Two former Marrister residents, Auld Glybbie (Johnie Irvine) and his sister Gracie (married name Poleson) both had large families, many of whom were also prolific. Their descendants now comprise a large percentage of Whalsay's population. Johnnie and Gracie's mother, Midder Janie, the renowned "howdie woman" (midwife), was put off her croft at Brough by the laird, after her husband died young, on the grounds that with three young children (there was another son, Lowrie) she would not be able to run the croft. The house they moved to at Marrister, called the Glybe (Glebe), as it was on land attached to the manse, was tiny. They were later allocated a croft at Saltness when the laird's farm was broken up in 1903. The Glybe was later occupied by an Irish woman called Nora who was married to or at least lived with Magnus Johnson from Symbister who had met her when in the merchant navy and who died relatively young: the house latterly became known as "Nora's". She was a Roman Catholic and had a small shrine with a cross down by the sea which she used as a sort of chapel. She survived into the 1950s.

Brough was named for the broch which was used to build the strip of twelve houses which replaced the original croft houses in the 1840s. Each house had a nickname, the one where the author's mother was born called "Dad Fit" (Stomp Foot). The last Peerie Laird of Lee was tricked out of his land by the Bruce laird of the day. Lee is just a single house so presumably the estate included Brough and the other nearby groups of houses – Houll, the Cready Knowe, the Creads and the Burns (where Alec Barclay kept the communal bull in the 1950s). The Lintihouse, where Robbie a' Lintihouse, a well-known genealogist lived, was named after an unsuccessful late 19th century experiment in growing flax to make linen cloth. The kirk and graveyard stand on a peninsula accessed across the Kirk Ayre, with a lighthouse at the end of it in Sutherness.

Challister is another old settlement where peerie lairds remained for some time after the Bruces arrived, not becoming absorbed into the Symbister Estate until 1823. Like Brough, the original crofts were replaced by new houses, in this case built around an open sided square. Nearby Vatshoull was also an old settlement, named from the nearby loch. Two brothers from here were exiled from the island in the 19th century for going to the Greenland whaling and their mother put a curse on the laird, the prophesy in which appears to have come true as the Bruce family has died out, their mansion became derelict and children now play in its grounds. Further north, Vevoe is a new township taken in from the scattald in the 19th century.

Skaw, at the north end of the island, has Britain's most northerly golf course, the course laid out in the early 1970s and the clubhouse built in 1996. An airstrip was also laid out here in the early 1970s, funded mainly by local subscriptions, but with the development of the car ferry system it was little used and is now defunct. Johnnie Bruce from Skaw was a renowned boat-builder and for a time in the 1960s shot seals for their skins along with a neighbour Alex Hutchison but this resource soon became depleted.

Isbister, the east farm in Old Norse, is thought to be the first place settled by the Vikings in Whalsay. According to John Stewart a chapel used to be located there at the Nishouse. Isbister has retained the old run-rig system whereby crofts are not consolidated but each has a share of the better land. They have their own public hall, built in 1909, the first one on the island.

Traewick is the only deserted village on the island. Its name derives from the Old Norse word for driftwood, "tre". At its peak in 1891 it had eleven houses and 55 people. During the First World War the Zetland County Council introduced a scheme to build roads using unemployed people, particularly fishermen. This was when the loop road around the island was constructed linking Symbister to Isbister, on to Brough and back to Symbister. Previously the made-up road had ended at the Spar Grind just east of Whitefield. The road was originally intended to go through Traewick but one local crofter, allegedly Robbie Anderson (some of his descendants deny this), refused to allow the road to go through his croft and it was re-routed through the scattald, well away from the Traewick houses, a third of a mile in most cases. District Council records show that a submission was made by the remaining six households in 1936 for a 500-yard link road to be built but nothing came of this. Gradually people left, the last family leaving in 1959. Across the road, opposite Traewick, lies Nuckrawater, where legend has it a monster lives, known as the "nykr". Allegedly, it often appeared as a horse and would carry people into the loch and drown them. Elsewhere in Shetland a similar beast was known as the Nyuggle and there is a loch called Nyuggleswater. The ponds to the east of Nuckrawater were used to collect ice to keep fish fresh while waiting to be shipped out on the *Earl of Zetland*.

At the end of the First World War, housing in Whalsay was generally of a very poor standard and tuberculosis was rife resulting in several deaths. There was also not enough of it, newly married couples generally having to stay with their parents and there was a lack of money for private house building. There had been some improvements in the housing stock around the turn of the 20th century. "Taekit" (straw) roofs had been replaced by wooden roofs covered with felt and tarred, at the same time houses being heightened to provide attic bedrooms with skylights and chimneys. The author can remember a survivor of the traditional style still with a straw roof and the full open fire in the early 1950s where Willie Irvine lived at East Hamister.

In 1945 a Labour government was elected which quickly started to apply its socialist policies. The first Council housing scheme was the Crudens built at Gardentown, just below the Hillhead, in the late 1940s. The Upper Crudens followed in 1955 and the North Park scheme in the early 1960s. The scheme at Saeter was built in the early 1970s using prefabricated kits built in Norway, followed by the Harlsdale houses built on the site of the former RAF camp. The Tripwell scheme dates from the 1980s and finally Norrendal in the 1990s.

Private house building continues apace having started to accelerate from the early 1960s as money flowed in from the revitalised fishing industry. The construction of sewerage schemes in most areas meant that houses could be built closer together since they no longer had to rely on septic tanks.

Whalsay has changed beyond recognition from the days when the lairds ruled the roost. Purely local affairs are now debated by the elected community council rather than decided by the laird's edict, although the SIC have the final say. There is now talk of a tunnel connecting Whalsay to the Mainland. What effect this removal of the island status would have on the people is difficult to predict, if it ever happens. But Whalsay has always adapted to changing circumstances, economic and social, in the past and will no doubt do so again.

Bibliography

James A. Anderson, 'The Shetland Germans', In The *Scots Magazine*, July 1987.

James A. Anderson, 'Madagascar: Revisiting a World War II Survival Saga' *Shetland Life*, April 2014.

Fojut, Noel, *A Guide to Prehistoric and Viking Shetland*, The Shetland Times Ltd., 1993.

C. A. Goodlad, *Shetland Fishing Saga*, The Shetland Times Ltd., 1971.

Graham, Laurence & Smith, Brian (Eds), *MacDiarmid in Shetland*, Shetland Library, 1992.

Hutchison, Loretta, 'A Whalsay Hero', *The New Shetlander* No.203.

Nicolson, James R., *Hay & Company, Merchants in Shetland*, 1982.

Nicolson, James R., *Shetland*, David & Charles, 1972.

Nicolson, James R., *Shetland Fishermen*, The Shetland Times Ltd., 1999.

Nicolson, James R., *Traditional Life in Shetland*, Robert Hale, 1978.

Peterson, James P., *The History of Shetland Football 1887-1987*, The Shetland Times Ltd., 1988.

Robson, Adam, *The Saga of the Earls*, The Shetland Times Ltd., 2002.

Smith, Brian (Ed.), *Shetland Archaeology*, The Shetland Times Ltd., 1985.

Stewart, John, *Folklore from Whalsay and Shetland*, Shetland Amenity Trust, 2005.

Stewart, John, *Shetland Place Names*, Shetland Library, 1987.

Tait, Jim, 'Hell Ships and Prison Camps/Fifteen Days Adrift on a Raft', *The Shetland Times*, 28th September, 2001.

Tait, Ian, *Shetland Vernacular Buildings*, The Shetland Times Ltd., 2012.

Turner, Val (Ed.), *The Shaping of Shetland*, Shetland Times Ltd., 1998.

The Royal Commission on the Ancient Monuments of Scotland, 12th Report, Volume III, Inventory of Shetland.

About the Author

The author was born on the island of Whalsay in the Shetland Islands. After graduating from Aberdeen University with an honours degree in geography he studied for a Diploma in education at Makerere University, Kampala, Uganda and then worked for two years as an education officer for the government of Kenya. He then moved to New Zealand where he qualified and worked as a town planner. Returning to Britain he became director of planning and environmental services with the Shetland Islands Council. After taking early retirement from the SIC in 1997, he returned to New Zealand and after serving as the district planner for Dunedin, set up his own town planning consultancy business.

Now retired, he divides his time between New Zealand and Shetland. He has previously published two travel books (*To the New 7 Wonders of the World* and *More New Wonders of the World*) and two novels, Malaika, set in Uganda at the time of Idi Amin's dictatorship and *Is Yun Dee, Robbie* (Is That You, Robbie) based on the banishment from Whalsay of his great-grandfather by the laird and a descendant's revenge on the last member of the laird's family. A keen traveller, he has visited 119 of the 195 countries in the world.

BV - #0027 - 060821 - C122 - 210/148/7 - PB - 9781910997345